GOD'S PLAN FOR THE SONS OF HAM

"A Future and a Hope"

CHIEF APOSTLE AARON B. CLAXTON
M.A, L.L.D, D.D., PhD

Foreword by Dr. Myles Munroe

GOD'S PLAN FOR THE SONS OF HAM
"A Future and a Hope"
Copyright © 1996 by Aaron B. Claxton

Printed in the
United States of America

Published by Kingdom Publishing, LLC
Odenton, Maryland

All rights reserved. No part of this book may be reproduced or transmitted in any form of by any means, electronic or mechanical, including photocopying, recording or by any information storage and retrieval system without written permission from the author, excerpt for the inclusion of brief quotations in a review.

All Scripture references are from the Authorized King James Version of the Bible, unless otherwise marked. Public Domain. References marked "NKJV" are from the New King James Version of the Bible @ copyright 1979,1980,1982 by Thomas Nelson, Inc., Nashville, Tennessee.

Cover Design: Erryn C. Claxton
ISBN Paperback: 978-1-947741-59-1
ISBN Ebook - 978-1-947741-60-7
Library of Congress Control Number: 2020915352

End Time Ministries of Christ Int., Inc.
P.O. Box 29180
Baltimore, MD 21205

DEDICATION

This book is dedicated to the memory of many generations of people of color (sons of Ham) all over the globe, who have suffered persecution, atrocities, indignities and inhumanness at the hands of their fair-skinned brethren. simply because of the color of their skin. We dedicate this book not only to their memory, but also to the brighter hope and future that our Creator-God has planned and purposed for us. (Jer. 29:11; Isa. 19:25)

ACKNOWLEDGEMENTS

We are thankful for this opportunity to express our appreciation to Pastor Clara Pyles for her many hours of tireless and unselfish labor of love which she put in on my book-hours of typing, retyping and making corrections at my request. Thank you, Pastor Pyles, and may God's richest blessings be yours, in your going out and coming in. We must, likewise, acknowledge the many hours of typing, corrections, advice and suggestions put in on this book by my lovely and precious wife of sixty years, Dr. Deborah J. Claxton.

TABLE OF CONTENTS

Foreword by Dr. Myles Munroe 6
Introduction 7
Chp 1 - Who Was Ham? Who Are His Sons? 15
Chp 2 - God's Merger and Blessing Plan 19
Chp 3 - Classical Africa and Eden 25
Chp 4 - Ham, First In Preeminence 31
Chp 5 - Africa, Mother of All Lands 37
Chp 6 - Origins of Racial Prejudice Against Africa 43
Chp 7 - God Favors Ham First 55
Chp 8 - God's Plan and Ham's Fall 65
Chp 9 - The Unfolding of God's Plan 71
Chp 10 - The Greatness and Downfall of Ham's Sons . 79
Chp 11 - Contemporary Trends in Restoration 95
Chp 12 - These Are No Coincidences! 103
Chp 13 - Ham – Helper of God's People 107
Chp 14 - Ham Blessed – Canaan Cursed 111
Chp 15 - Black Champions of the Church 115
Chp 16 - Three African Popes 123
Chp 17 - Conclusion 127
Bibliography 130

FOREWORD BY DR. MYLES MUNROE

Understand that the greatest enemy of many is ignorance, it is imperative that the light of knowledge be shed on all areas of this darkness by the Truth that sets men free. Apostle Claxton, in his book, God's Plan For the Sons of Ham, is a valuable source of light for all who wish to dispel the darkness of centuries of misunderstanding and abuse concerning a whole race of valuable people. May you discover treasure in this book and share them with others as we strive together to walk in the light.

Sincerely Yours,
Dr. Myles Munroe

INTRODUCTION

At the time of this writing we can say, of a truth, that God is indeed smiling upon his people Egypt (the Black man, Isaiah 19:25) as he continues to loose us from the bonds of our Gentile oppressors.

In 1986, I was in Benin City, Nigeria, West Africa. I was there for the dedication of the great Faith Cathedrome, pastored by Archbishop Benson Idahosa. He is a Nigerian preacher raised up from humble ranks to become undoubtedly the mightiest preacher on the continent of Africa in our day. He has preached out five thousand churches and oversees five million people. He has had mighty miracles wrought in his ministry, and has raised at least eight people from the dead. I was consecrated to the bishopric in that city by the hand of this great man of God in 1989.

There is, of course, a tremendous revival breaking forth in Africa today, Surely, princes (royal leaders) are coming out of "Egypt" today, out from among black people (Psalm 68:32). You see, the original meaning of the word Egypt is black! Psalm 68:31 speaks about the black man. Egypt is really the Greek form of the word *Chemii,* from the name of Ham (or *Kemet*).

Only a few days ago (May, 1994) as my darling wife and I visited Uganda and saw the source of the White Nile there, we became aware that we were truly treading near the birthplace of humanity. As we traveled by car from Uganda, en route to Nairobi, Kenya, we passed near the approximate location of the Garden of Eden which is in Tanzania. We were blessed to be in Nairobi on May 30th, 1994, and to share in the 30th celebration of their Independence Day, the day of their deliverance as captives from the British Crown or Gentile colonial ruler!

At this very time a historic "African American Leadership Summit" is convening in our city of Baltimore, Maryland, under the auspices of the NAACP. Their agenda will deal with "Black on Black" crime, jobs (economics) and the quality of life of African Americans. One attendee told a news reporter on camera that the two things he expected to see accomplished at the Summit were "new possibilities and hope" for the African American community.

As we look back, we see that just a few weeks ago (May, 1994) one of the last walls of bondage of black people came down, when Nelson Mandela, former political prisoner, became South Africa's first Black president in over three hundred years! Of a truth, the Word of God is being fulfilled in our eyes, "Princes (royal leaders) are coming out of Egypt (from among the ranks of Black people) and Ethiopia (burnt-face people) are soon (now) stretching forth their hands unto God" (Psalm 68:31). Praise God, we are living to witness that *"There is hope in your (our) future, says the Lord"* (Jeremiah 31:17).

We are most grateful for the thorough work of research and compiling done by Anthony Browder, in his researching out of the accurate knowledge and truth about the true history and great contributions of the Hamitic people to the whole human history and civilization *(Nile Valley Contrib. to Civ., Exploding the Myths. Vol 1).*

Whereas Mr. Browder began with the Nile Valley and documented the great inventions and discoveries of the ancient people therein- the Nubians, Ethiopians and Chemi (Egyptians); dating back some three thousand years before Christ, we would like to go back even further in documenting the tremendous works of these great and mighty people of color!

Mr. Browder documented the contributions of the above-named peoples as originators of embalming, medicine, astronomy, mathematics, architecture, the calendar, the clock, agriculture, astrology, religious architecture, well organized religion, physics, chemistry, geology, meteorology, music and art.

He began with the great and mighty ancient Nubian (Sudanese people), who are said to have founded the oldest Monarchy in the world. This is far from the Bible record which cites Nimrod as the first kingdom and city builder on earth (Genesis 10) three thousand years before Christ. Nimrod was the firstborn of Cush.

Whereas Alex Haley's "Roots" in West Africa with the African slave trade and whereas Anthony Browder's great research and books go back to ancient Nubia (relative to the beginnings of the great civilizations of people of color, to history and to the Western civilization), let us begin with the biblical account, despite the fact that ancient Nubia, Ethiopia and Kemet far predate Moses' writing of the creation narrative.

Although Moses wrote around 1400 B.C., about a creation that happened about 4000 B.C., let us take note that Elohim, the great and only Creator knew and knows the end from the beginning, saying, *"My counsel shall stand, and I will do all my pleasure"* (Isaiah 46:10). Let us consider that in the creative narrative that Adam (red man) was sculpted out of soil that was a dark, reddish-brown color, and that rivers relating to both Havilah (the second son of Cush) and Ethiopia (Cush himself) are named as being in the vicinity of the Garden of Eden. Where was Eden? It was on the continent of Classical Africa, the central, eastern part of original Africa.

What am I saying? I am simply stating that Anthony Browder's account does not differ greatly from the biblical account of the origins of civilization, as we know it today.

Let's look further. The Bible so closely links the Black man with the beginnings of human history and civilization, that we read the following in Micah 5:6: *"…the land of Assyria…the land of Nimrod in the entrances thereof…"* The Bible tells us that Nimrod, Cush's first son was a *"a mighty one in the earth."*

He was a mighty hunter before the Lord. And the beginning of his kingdom was Babel…in the land of Shinar (Sumer)" Genesis 10:8-10). In Shinar the offspring of Nimrod and Shem, especially Ashur, mixed freely. The Hamites were more numerous, more active, more creative and more proactive than the offspring of Shem and Japheth. It was here that the ancient Sumerians, who were bronze-colored Babylonians, founded the world's first business civilization!

As a "mighty hunter," Nimrod had to be associated with the ancient site near the southernmost province of ancient Kemet (Egypt) called Ta-Seli, which means, *The Land of the Bow,* referring to their skilled archers!

If we look upon the ancient super-race of black or dark-skinned people as one people, although they all descended from Ham through four separate sons, i.e., Cush, Mizraim, Phut and Canaan, then we can see at least some of them shining in great glory in the earliest days of mankind, i.e., the Nubians, the Ethiopians, the Chemii (people of Kemet) and the Phoenicians, earlier known as the Sidonians, who were Canaanites. The latter originated city-states, not the Greeks, as is commonly believed.

Isaiah the prophet records Jehovah's pronouncements upon both Nubia and Egypt. He writes: *"Woe to the land shadowing with wings, which is beyond the rivers of Ethiopia."*

This is where the Blue (Ethiopia) and White (Uganda) Nile Rivers join at Khartoum is Sudan, formerly Nubia, and the two branches appear to be "wings" hovering over upper Kemet or Egypt. Because of Nubia's superior might in warfare, and because of Egypt's superlative wisdom above other nations, they became lifted up in pride. That is why both were cast down and are poor, groveling nations today!

The Aim of This Book

We aim to show from Scripture and related historical writings that Afro-Asiatic people of the world were the ones with whom God began human civilization and that the seed of Ham (Cush, Mizraim and Canaan) with the seed of Shem (especially through Abraham), for the purpose of bestowing special blessings upon them, by which He would bless the world. We also aim to show that both groups (Ham and Shem) were severely punished by God in history for their sins; and finally, that there is a great hope of restoration and blessing planned for Ham and Israel in their latter end.

Introduction

A further aim of our book is to expose our readers to truthful facts of history and of the Bible, so as to move the thinking of Blacks about themselves (Blacks and non-blacks) from a negative viewpoint to a positive one.

Let us diverge slightly here to state our reasons for writing this book. Those reasons are as follows:

1. My love for my people, the Black man, in America, Africa and throughout the world;
2. Questions I had about our history of suffering, slavery, second-class citizenship and what the future holds for us as a people;
3. My deep love for my people and my desire to see them saved, is no less than St. Paul's desire to see Israel, his people in the Bible, saved (Romans 10:1-2), nor the present-day desire of Dr. Morris Cerullo, a Jew, to see his people saved.
4. God's prophetic word that came to me in 1990, and subsequently that I would write many books, which was a confirmation of a "knowing" which I already had in my heart.

We need to realize that European scholars and the Catholic church recast secular history and the Bible in the light of themselves, so as to give both a decidedly *Eurocentric* flavor, and a halo over themselves. This view has been strengthened in the past fifty plus years in America through the news and entertainment media, especially through movies and T.V. People of color throughout the world and in Africa itself have been sorely crippled mentally and emotionally by the constant bombardment of negative stereotypes and lies foisted upon us by our Caucasian masters—especially since the 1700s.

It is far past time that we Blacks know the truth about ourselves in world history, and that non-blacks know and acknowledge the same. The truth is that Adam, God's first created human being, was the dark red color of the soil out of which he was formed. God pronounced His creation on the sixth day, "very good," yet whites for centuries taught themselves and Blacks that "Black is bad, negative and inferior!" Currently, there is a massive book out entitled *The Bell Curve* by Charles Murray. This book resulted from extensive research in the field of education and claims to have "proof" that Blacks are "intellectually inferior" to whites.

CHAPTER ONE
WHO WAS HAM? WHO ARE HIS SONS?

Ham seems to have been the second son of Noah, based on the following scripture passages: Genesis 5:32, 6:9, AND 9:18. There are some Bible scholars who believe that Ham was Noah's youngest, or third son.

Ham's name in Hebrew means sun-burnt. Smith's Bible Dictionary (Revised Edition) says the following about Ham:

> *Ham (warm) (Egyptian chem, dark). One of the sons of Noah (Gen. vi, 10) …settled in Africa…and also sent many branches into Asia (Canaanites). There is no ancient name so well preserved* and located. Ham is identified with JUPITER, AMMON,

and also ZEUS, because both words are derived from a root meaning hot, fervent, or sunburnt. For the last 3000 years the world has been mainly indebted for its advancement to the Semitic races; but before this period, the descendants of Ham—Egypt and Babylon—led the way as the pioneers in art, literature and science. Mankind at the present day lies under infinite obligations to the genius and industry of those early ages, more especially for alphabetic writing, weaving cloth, architecture, astronomy, plastic art, sculpture, navigation and agriculture. The art of painting is also represented, and music indirectly, by drawings of instruments.

Unger's Bible Dictionary says the following about Ham:

> ...the name of Ham alone, of the three sons of Noah... is known to have been given to a country (Psalm 78:51; 105:23; 106:22).

The sons of Ham, biblically speaking were Cush, Mizriam, Phut and Canaan (Genesis 10:6). The sons of Ham today would be the darker-skinned peoples of the earth who migrated from various parts of Africa, Asia and Palestine to settle throughout the world, including the isles of the seas.

We will see in this book that the original architects of human civilization were dark-skinned people of great genius who sprang out of the continent of **Africa (Akebu-lan, "Mother of all Lands")**, as did Adam! We will be refreshed upon learning that the whole backdrop of the Old Testament narrative was largely acted out on the continent of Classical Africa, on a stage with "actors" who were either dark complexioned or Black (Egyptians, Ethiopians, Israelites and Canaanites).

Is it any wonder the Shullamite lover of King Solomon declared, *"I am black but beautiful (like Solomon)?"* (Song of Solomon 1:5). Is there any wonder that the eight century Greek poet, Homer, referred to Africans as "Ethiopia's faultless men"? Surely, in that day, racial prejudice based on one's color was unknown. People were given credit for their accomplishments based on their abilities, yea, "On the content of their character and not on the color of their skin"!

We do not want to indicate, by any means, that the sons of Ham, of black people, were better than any other people found in history or in the Bible. What we do want to point out from scripture and other forms of historical writings which have been written primarily by men of color, is that God had a definite plan in mind with regard to the offspring of Ham. A plan by definition, from the World Book Dictionary, (the third connotation) is: *a project or definite purpose.* We are saying that God did have a project or definite purpose in mind with regard to the offspring of Ham and the offspring of Shem, in linking one with another in the Bible, and that this linkage would bring about great blessings to the human family.

CHAPTER TWO
GOD'S MERGER AND BLESSING PLAN

Let us look more closely at God's "merger plan" between the offspring of Shem and Ham.
We are presented with a classic picture of this truth with the family of Jacob and his wives. For those who may not know the story, Jacob was sent by his father Isaac to his mother's brother's house (uncle Laban) to select a wife. Jacob fell in love with the younger of two sisters whose name was Rachel. The older sister was named Leah.

After Jacob had worked the agreed-upon seven years to earn the right to marry his beloved Rachel, his uncle deceived him by substituting the older daughter, Leah, in the marriage tent on the wedding night. For this reason, Jacob was forced to work an additional seven years for the younger daughter whom he loved.

After Leah bore Jacob three sons, and Rachel had borne him none because of barrenness, the Lord began to orchestrate His merger plan of which we have spoken. Laban gave Rachel his handmaiden named Bilhah, who was definitely Hamitic and probably Canaanite.

Do you remember that the Mesopotamian area was called *"the land of Nimrod (Cushite)"* (Micah 5:6)? Rachel proceeded to give her handmaiden Bilhah to Jacob and by her he begot two sons, Dan and Naphtali.

In the spirit of competition Leah proceeded to give Jacob her handmaiden, Zilpah (also Hamitic) who promptly bore him two sons, Gad and Asher. Therefore, we see that **four** of the sons of Jacob and the tribes that descended from them were part Hamite.

Let us observe that Judah married a Canaanite wife, had three sons by her, and two of them died. The oldest son married a Canaanite maiden named Tamar, but she became widowed at his death (Genesis 38: 1-12). Judah's wife died and he unknowingly cohabited with his own daughter-in-law Tamar, thinking she was a harlot, because she had disguised herself as such. She conceived and bore him twins. (Genesis 38:14-30). This union produced a fifth tribe of Israel that has a Hamitic connection.

Joseph, Jacobs son by Rachel, was sold as a slave in Egypt and after many years was blessed by God to become the prime minister of the nation. At that time Joseph married an Egyptian wife, Asenath, who bore him two sons, named Ephraim and Manasseh. These two sons' offspring later came to be called "half-tribes" had a Hamitic connection.

"The crossbreeding between Hebrews and Blacks went on, despite laws against it (Deuteronomy 7:3, Nehemiah 31:17-18, Ezra 9:1-15 and 10:1-44). Such laws existed for the maintenance of religious purity, not racial purity, because Jews were already a mixed people before departing Negro-Egypt. *This is why some historians think of Jews to be of Negro ancestry. Strabo went on to say that Jews living in western Judea were partly African* (Egyptian). *The Roman Taction supported this by saying, "Jews were of the Ethiopian race"'* (Ref. The Black Biblical Heritage, p. 55).

"*The modern white Jews receive much of their praise, culture and popularity from the history of the early ancient black Jews, who were the original Hebrews. The bright complected Jews contributed nothing to the early Hebrew development, nor were they present during the Exodus from Egypt under Moses or the invasion of Canaan. The white Jews appeared about one hundred years after the death of Solomon (II Kings 5:27). Abraham, Isaac, Jacob and their descendants until the book of Second Kings, were black-skinned people, largely mixed with the African (Hamitic) element.*"

The Illustrated Dictionary & Concordance of the Bible, published by The Reader's Digest Association says:

> *"Scholarly, biblical research reveals that 'Caleb the son of Jephunnah the Kenizzite' was indeed a man of color, a Black man (Joshua 14:14). Kenezzites are described as 'One of the non-Israelite peoples who inhabited southern Canaan during the period of the patriarchs"* (Genesis 15:19). *Their ancestor Kenaz, appears to be a son of Eliphaz, the eldest* son of Esau (whose first wife was a Hittite) (Genesis 36:15, 41; 1 Chronicles 1:53). An important Kenizzite family, the Caleb clan (Numbers 32:12), conquered Hebron (Joshua 14:6, 12-14) and became a part of Judah according to the commandment of God to Joshua (15:13) ...Caleb, whose name means dog was, in fact, a proselyte to the Jewish faith. He was of the seed of Canaan and therefore of Ham. He was one of the twelve spies sent by Moses.... to scout the land of Canaan (Numbers 13;6). Ephraim was the son of Joseph and his Egyptian mother, Asenath. When the spies returned, Caleb advised an immediate conquest of Canaan (Num. 13:30); his view was supported only by Joshua, the representative of the tribe of Ephraim (Numbers 14:6-8).

This means that both of these leaders who led Israel in the Conquest of Canaan were men of **Hamitic** extraction! They represent a perfect picture of the Black and the Jew (Ham and Shem) flowing together in the purpose of God!

According to Joshua 15:17; Judges 1:13 the brothers Caleb and Othniel are sons of Kenaz. I Chronicles 2:18 lists Caleb as the son of Hezron the son of Perez, one of the twins born to Judah and Tamar (Genesis 38:27-30); I Chronicles 2-4) (quoted from same source immediately above).

Tamar, by the way, was Judah's Canaanite daughter-in-law, who, along with her twin sons, Perez and Zerah, are named in the genealogy of Jesus Christ (Matthew 1:3)!

Allow me to diverge at this point to relate a personal experience we believe to be germane to our discussion. We have posited somewhere in our books that the Canaanites, the original inhabited of Palestine, who were sons of Ham, were black or dark-skinned people. During my wife's and my third visit to Israel, around 1985, we spent a few minutes talking to a small group of dark-skinned citizens of that land in the vicinity of Jericho. They resembled any medium brown-skin African-American, but their accent was either Arabic or Hebraic. Their hair was finer textured than most African-Americans. Upon questioning this group of young men about how long their people had lived there, it became apparent to me that they were not really certain. However, one of them offered that he thought it had been about four hundred years. Afterwards it dawned on me that we had just possible held discussions with some of the offspring of some of the original inhabitants of the land of Canaan!

The major aim of my book then, is to show from Scripture and from related historical writings that the Afro-Asiatic people or the Afro-Edenic people of the world, the people found in Eden in the Bible, were the ones with whom God began human civilization. God had a definite plan in mind in linking the seed of Ham, with the seed of Shem, that is, Cush, Mizraim and Canaan. These are the three sons of Ham, whom God linked with the seed of Shem, especially through Abraham, Jacob, Judah, Joseph, Moses and David for the purpose of bestowing special blessings upon them, by which He would bless the entire world. Both groups, Ham and Shem, were greatly blessed of God in the beginning, and both were severely punished by Him in history for their gross wickedness and evil against God.

Finally, there is a great hope of restoration and blessings planned by God both for Ham and Israel, in their latter end. May the Lord bless that which we are endeavoring to impart into the hearts of the readers, and may people of color, yea Black people, all over the world, upon reading the contents of this book, get fresh hope and a fresh, positive outlook for the future. There are great things lying in store for us according to the word of God!

CHAPTER THREE
CLASSICAL AFRICA AND EDEN

Adam, God's first human creation, as recorded in the book of Genesis, chapters one and two, was taken out of the dust of the ground, that is, regarding his physical being. My precious wife and I have visited Africa, in various parts of Nigeria. Most recently, we visited East Africa, in both Uganda and Kenya, near Tanzania. We were able to see that the soil in both places was usually a dark reddish-brown color. We also found in Uganda and Kenya that the ground was a very rich, deep, black color. We know then that Adam (the Hebrew pronounces it Ad-ham) was dark reddish-brown in color. We are also told that the Hebrew word for Adam actually means *red* or *red man*. In any event, we know that Adam was a dark-skinned man.

As we look down the line of time when the flood came, after wickedness had increased and multiplied upon the earth, we see that God preserved one righteous man and his family. His name was Noah.

Noah's name means rest. He had three sons, Shem, Ham and Japheth. The Bible tells us that only eight souls were preserved out of the tremendous flood of judgement that God sent upon the earth, Noah and his wife and his three sons and their wives. You will find it in the third chapter of first Peter. As we go further, we will find what the Bible says concerning these three sons of Noah in the ninth chapter of the book of Genesis, that from them the whole earth was overspread or repopulated.

At this point I am going to draw upon the testimony of the Reverend Cain Hope Felder, Ph.D., professor of New Testament Languages and Literature at Howard University, Washington, D.C. He is also the General Editor of the original African Heritage Study Bible. I am going to draw some statements from him that will bear out something I am saying about men of color, men of the African-Edenic area. We will also draw from other studies, such as a book called *People of Color in the Bible*, written by William Gilbert Emanuel, a minister of the Gospel, lecturer, and author.

We must be made aware of this fact: Africa originally was one total land mass, taking in the area where the Tigris and Euphrates Rivers flow. The Bible speaks, in Genesis chapter two, about the four rivers and the river heads that surrounded the Garden of Eden which was in the east of Eden. The two rivers that God speaks most thoroughly about were connected with Havilah, who was a son of Cush, a black man. These two river heads were connected with Ethiopia.

Scholars have determined that these two rivers are none other than the two heads of the Nile River—the Blue Nile and the White Nile. Again, having visited east Africa recently, we saw one source of the Nile in Uganda. The other source is in Ethiopia. The two heads come together and form one river in Nubia, i.e. Sudan.

The Nubians were people of very dark skins occupying the southern part of what we know today as Egypt. Some of the most brilliant minds known to mankind came from this area, in the very beginning. The late president of Egypt, Anwar Sadat was a Nubian.

The Nile flows from south to north, originating in the heart of central Africa. It flows northerly, then through the Sudan, on through Egypt and empties into the Mediterranean Sea. We need to understand that prior to 1859 or 1869, Africa was one complete land mass. The northern most portion we call the area Ur of the Chaldees. The Babylonians came from that area and Abraham came from that area. Hamites, Shemites and Japhethites all dwelt in that area prior to all nations being scattered from the Tower of Babel (Genesis 11). Havilah settled in that area. Havilah is one of the sons of Cush, a black man. Cush is the Hebrew word meaning *black, dark or sunburnt.* This was one land mass until the Suez Canal was *opened around 1869.*

During the Second World War, the upper area of classical Africa, the Palestinian area, began to be called the Middle East. Originally it was all Africa. All this area was also called **Eden**. The word Eden, from the original language, means *pleasant* or *delight.* Oftentimes in history Israel has been called, *"God's delightsome land."* In the book of Daniel chapter 11, Palestine is called, *"God's pleasant land."* The whole area of Africa was called Eden, the place of delight or the place of pleasantness. God planted a garden eastward in Eden and scholars today have concluded that this would be somewhere around Tanzania, in East Africa. The most ancient fossils of mankind have been found in this area. This was reported in 1988 and through the early 90's, in some of the major magazines in America and Europe. Time magazine, Newsweek, etc. began to report that archaeologists had found a fossil which could be called Mother Eve.

We have now established the aforementioned point from both secular sources and from the Bible. Perhaps we need to go to the Bible and read that you may know that we are not making this up, but it is indeed recorded in the Word of God.

Let us therefore read from Genesis 2:7-14, the King James version. The Word of the Lord says: *"And the Lord formed man from the dust of the ground, and breathed into his nostrils the breath of life; and man became a living soul.*

Classical Africa and Eden

And the Lord God planted a garden eastward in Eden; and there he put the man whom he had formed. And out of the ground made the Lord God to grow every tree that is pleasant to the sight, and for food; the tree of life also in the midst of the garden, and the tree of knowledge of good and evil. And a river went out of Eden to water the garden; and from thence parted, and became in to four heads. The name of the first is Pison; that is it which compasseth the whole land of Havilah, where there is gold; And the gold of that land is good; there is bdellium and the onyx stone. And the name of the second is Gihon: the same is it that compasseth the whole land of Ethiopia." (Take note that at one time all of Africa was called Ethiopia, or it has been called Libya; it has been called by these various names.)

"And the name of the third river is Hiddekel; that is it which goeth toward the east of Assyria. And the fourth river is Euphrates." These four rivers heads were none other than the two branches of the Nile river, (as believed by some), and the Tigris and Euphrates rivers. All who grew up in Africa in the beginning were dark-skinned people, whether they were Hamitic or Semitic, they were dark-skinned peoples.

God's Plan for the Sons of Ham

CHAPTER FOUR
HAM, FIRST IN PREEMINENCE

What we need to know from Genesis ten, is that among all the sons of Noah, the Hamites predominated in number. History testifies that they predominated in activity, and creativity. Verse six of chapter ten reads thusly: *"And the sons of Ham: Cush, and Mizraim, and Phut, and Canaan. And the sons of Cush; Seba, and Dedan. And Cush begat Nimrod; he began to be a mighty hunter in the earth."*

We find in a Bible dictionary that the name Nimrod means *Builder*. The Bible says, in Genesis chapter 10 verse 8: *"And Cush begat Nimrod and he began to be a mighty one in the earth."* The word for mighty one in Hebrew is *Gibbor, one who is awesome in his ability or his works*. The Bible goes on to say that he was *a "mighty hunter"* before the Lord. In other words, his name became a proverb. His name became a buzz word in that day. Everybody in the land of Shinar knew the name of Nimrod. He was in fact, the ruler and the leader there.

The Word goes on to tell us, *"And the beginning of his Kingdom was Babel, Erech, and Accad, and Calneh in the land of Shinar."* What we are led to see then, is that the first kingdom or monarchy upon the earth was begun by and through a black man, even Nimrod. He became a great builder. The man became so great, we are told in historical records, that his name began to ring around the known world, after the scattering of the people, after the confusion of tongues by God in the 11th chapter of Genesis, where He dispersed the offspring of the sons of Noah. They were the sons of Shem, Ham and Japheth who had been living in this area, the land of Shinar. The Lord then scattered them throughout the earth. It is pretty well documented that the sons of Japheth, according to the 10th chapter of the book of Genesis, were indeed the original Gentiles. When you speak of Gentiles proper you are speaking of the sons of Japheth.

We read in the Word of the Lord, *"Now these are the generations of the sons of Noah, Shem, Ham and Japheth and unto them were sons born after the flood. The sons of Japheth were Gomer, Ashkenaz and Riphath, and Togarmah, and the sons of Javan: Elishah, and Tarshish, Kittim and Dodanim. By these were the isles of the Gentiles divided in their land, every tongue, after their families in their nations."* So, the word Gentiles in one place in the Bible speaks of those, who were **coast-land dwellers,** and in another place, they were spoken of as **isles.** These are the people who went up into what we now know as Eastern and Western Europe, primarily, and settled. They later came to be known as the Germans, Russians, Polish, British, France, Scandinavians, etc. (Genesis 10:1-5).

Now that we have consulted the Bible, the written Word of God, as our first source to show that the beginning of city building, kingdoms and civilization was indeed begun by the sons of Ham and especially through Cush, i.e. Nimrod, I want to go on to say that Nimrod's fame became so great that men began to worship him. Some scholars believe that the Madonna and child were black in the beginning, and really began with a story of Nimrod dying and "coming back to life," and his mother "conceiving" him. Some scholars believe that the whole idea of mother and child began with Nimrod. Therefore, you can find evidences of worship of Nimrod as the child of the Madonna all over the world, in the far East, eastern Europe and throughout Arabia. It is not for us to say whether these scholars are correct or not, but at least it is something we have found in secular history referring to this tremendous black man and his great fame that went throughout the world.

We want to turn to some secular sources, in order to draw from them statements relative to human civilization, and where it began. Let us now quote from *Exploding the Myths, Volume One, Nile Valley Contributions to Civilization,* Anthony T. Browder. He has done quite a bit of research on Africa and Ethiopia. He is a graduate of Howard University in Washington, D.C. in the field of humanities. On page 71 of Browder's book, he speaks of the historical accomplishments of Kemet, (Egypt):

> *Modern technology has created rockets which have taken man to the moon and has launched satellites to explore the farthest regions of the galaxy. The marvelous advances in computer science now make it possible to compress the contents of libraries into disks no larger than a long-playing record. Despite these technological advances, modern man cannot recreate the technology that built the great pyramids or mummified the kings of Kemet. Kemet is the name of ancient Egypt in the original tongue. It comes from the name Ham. The admiration of the accomplishments of Kemet has given rise to an entire field of study named in its honor called Egyptology. The unearthing of her "priceless" treasures has brought wealth and fame to archaeologists and their financial backers. No nation in the history of civilization has had a greater influence on the arts and sciences than Kemet. It is there that one can still find the only remaining one of the seven wonders of the world. What the scholars of color have determined is that the original civilization and accomplishments therein (in*

Kemet) began in Nubia. They were then carried back to Egypt, which would be somewhere to the North of Nubia, and southeasterly to Ethopia.

As we look at some of the things Anthony Browder showed us that Egypt gave to the world through documented evidence, we find that this dates back to over three thousand years ago. We find that the Kemetic people were the originators of such fields as mathematics, medicine, physics, etc. The great multi-talented scholar of that ancient time was named **Imhotep**, a great physician, builder and architect. Medicine, which included embalming, is a science that men have not been able to discover or duplicate today. Astronomy, the science of searching out the heavens and being able to name all the heavenly bodies, touching on the galaxies and their movements, was also discovered by the ancient black people of Kemet. They discovered mathematics and architecture. When I say mathematics, I am not talking about simple arithmetic. I am talking about advanced mathematics—geometry, the use of logarithms and such things. Experts in that field will know what I am talking about. In other words, the hard sciences have Kemet, Ethiopia and Nubia to thank for the foundations that were laid there. Then there was religious architecture, a well-organized ancient religious system, physics and chemistry which the people of Kemet invented. I wonder if the word chemistry has its roots in the word *Chemii,* which is what the people of the land of Ham or particularly Egypt were called? Other sciences and arts discovered in Kemet were geology, meteorology, and music—to name a few of the great innovations and discoveries that were made by these ancient black people, over three thousand years ago!

CHAPTER FIVE
AFRICA, MOTHER OF ALL LANDS

The Original African Heritage Study Bible states:

It is chiefly the illiterates, the undereducated, and racially biased who refute the fact that the earliest and first human (Homo sapiens) was discovered in the area of what is known today as Africa. And that the place at that time was called Eden. From this point humankind migrated throughout the world. Facts have been gathered from the land of Kenya, East Africa, in the place of Lake Rudolph, where Richard Leakey, was co-leader of the expedition that found the bones of the earliest man. Any history book of academic repute sanctions the African connection to ancient secular and religious civilization. Because of abundant facts and from African/Edenic roots. The opening scenario of the Holy Scriptures talks of Egypt and Ethiopia. At one time Egypt and Ethiopia are synonymous. The term Egypt was once used to mean all of Africa, which was called the "Land of Ham"(Psalm 105).

According to the ancient historians Flavious Josephus, Celus, Putarch, Tacitus, Eusebius, and Diodorius, the original Hebrews were a group of Ethiopians and Egyptians who were forced to leave Egypt and migrate to Canaan. Even today, we accept the scholarship from Cheikh Diop and Gerald Massey, who affirm the African world and were originally black-skinned peoples. Manetho's history of the Egyptians, the only surviving one from an identifiable Egyptian historian, corroborates this impression. It is without doubt that if the Jewish clan of seventy persons were not black upon entering Egypt to see Joseph, it is certain that they were black when they departed under the leadership of Moses. Also, it is important to note if there were any literate persons among them other than Moses himself, their spoken and written language and literature would have been Egyptian when they left. As a matter of speaking, the Hebrew language did not exist at that time.

This land was a massive continent and not always called Africa. Among the many names, Akebu-Lan is the oldest and the most indigenous, and means

"Mother of Mankind' or 'Garden of Eden.' This name was used by the Moors, Nubians, Numidians, "Khart-Haddans (Carthagenians, and Ethiopians). The current name Africa is a misnomer, adopted by almost everyone today. The name Africa was given to this continent by the ancient Romans. Other names that refer to Africa are Kemet, Libya, Ortegia, Corphye, Egypt, Ethiopia and/or Sudan, Olympia, Hesperia, Ocenia, Ta-Merry.

In 1675 B.C. neither the name Jew nor Negro existed. The term Negro was given to the Blacks as they left Africa for the slave ships (ca. 1500 A.D.). This is when the name 'Negroland. was used. This is strictly a term coined by the Portuguese which means 'black'. It has nothing to do with a race of people. Using this term saved people from having to call the slave Cushites, Ethiopians, or Abssynians, which they are sometimes called in the Bible. But literate England and Portugal knew quite well that these peoples whom they captured and chained were the same that were spoken of in the Holy Scriptures, and knew they were the first ones to carry and establish Christianity and Judaism in Africa, northeast Africa and Europe. Western biases have so thwarted the history of the black race that it takes great study and research to unravel this maze of myths and confusion…

From the Introduction to the Bible:

> *The Original African Heritage Study Bible has been prepared to bring order and clarity to the confusion, truth to the lie, and light to the darkness about ancient biblical truths. Our first task is to use biblical evidence, supportive academic references, and common sense to show that the ancestral home of man (Adam), humanity's common ancestor, was in Africa, the land associated with the beginnings of Eden in the Bible Readers today must understand that in biblical times 'Africa' included much of what European maps have come to call the 'Middle East. 'Remember, the name Africa is actually of Latin origin and was imposed on that great continent by European explorers.*

In the Introduction to *The Original African Heritage Study Bible,* written by the General Editor, who is none other than the Reverend Cain Hope Felder, PhD., professor of New Testament Languages and Literature at Howard University, Washington, D.C., beginning on page 103, there are five maps showing the original land known as Africa. Africa was not the name of that original land. Africa in the Bible was known as the land of Ham. It included what is known as classical Africa or ancient Africa. That would be both the large land mass on the lower portion and the upper portion, because the two land masses were connected, which would take in what men now call the Middle East. The land masses were separated in 1859 through 1869 when the Suez Canal was built. The scholars in this study Bible seek to pinpoint the actual location of the origin of modern humans, in other words, where the Garden of Eden was located. I have already told you that it was in East Central Africa and that it was near what we would now call Tanzania.

Let us quote from page 107 of the Introduction to the Original Africa Heritage Study Bible. It says:

The birth of the creation of the first human (homo-sapiens) took place in the heart of biblical Africa which was called at that time Eden. The three rivers spoken of in Genesis 2:10-14, verify human existence in this area. To substantiate the biblical story of creation, archaeologists and scientists confirm that the oldest form of human life has been discovered around the Olduaivue Gorge in present day Tanzania. It was from this point that humankind found a way to other parts of the known world. The first move was toward northeast Africa, the "Middle East", and from there into Asia and Europe. Therefore, during the Bible days when civilization was high in Kemet (Egypt), there was little known activity on the continent we know today as Europe. Civilization came late to the Caucasians of the north, and that which came was brought forth Akebu-lan (Africa), 'the Mother of all Lands."

Akebu-lan was evidently the ancient name of Africa that the People from that part of the world, the Afro-Edenic people, the Afro-Asiatic people, called that land.

CHAPTER SIX
THE ORIGINS OF RACIAL PREJUDICE AGAINST AFRICANS

The idea that blacks are low class people, inferior people, less important people than Europeans or Caucasians, began with some European scholars. *(Nile Valley Contributions to Civilization, p. 19)*. This was around the 1700s when slavery was under way, having begun in North Africa, between the Arabs and the Portuguese. They began to export human cargo out of Africa, black-skinned people to be sold in Europe and in other parts of the world, especially in the Americas.

There has been a tremendous cover-up. Some horrendous lies, distortions and perversions have been visited upon true history, to distort the picture, to blind the eyes of people even unto this day, that black people were not as great as they really were in the beginning. This has been done deliberately out of a spirit of *ethnocentrism*. Ethnocentrism is a word that comes out of the field of Sociology or the study of Ethnology. It means *to place one's culture above another culture,* or to say one's culture is better than someone else's culture. Ethnology is the study of certain groups of people within races.

On page v of the Introduction of *The Original African Heritage Study Bible* under the heading, "A Foundation of Truth," we find the following statements:

> *For too long in the history of Western civilization, persons of African descent have been stereotyped in negative ways which have caused them to question not only their own identity but also their part in God's plan of salvation. Afrocentricity, the idea that Africa and persons of African descent must be understood as making significant contributions to world civilization as proactive subjects within history, is the methodology with which the Original African Heritage Study Bible endeavors to reappraise ancient biblical traditions. The impressive number of volumes which have appeared in the past few years attempting to engage in 'corrective historiography' attest to the fact that it is no longer enough to limit the discussion to 'black theology' or even African theology; instead, Africa, her people, nations, and cultures, must be acknowledged as making primary, direct contributions*

to the development of Christianity. The purpose of the Original African Heritage Study Bible is to interpret the Bible as it relates specifically to persons of African descent and thereby to foster an appreciation of the multiculturalism and inclusiveness, seeking to bring forth the truth from a story which has had many dubious interpretations…Recently in America and in Africa, there has developed a proliferation of books and pamphlets which represent a resurgence of what may be called Afrocentric approaches to the Bible… Ref. (Ibid p. VIII)

The 'curse of Ham' is a post-biblical myth. In Gen. 9:18-29, Ham is not the recipient of a curse. The text explicitly says, 'Let Canaan be cursed.' Furthermore, Ham does not mean 'black' in Hebrew, it translates literally as 'hot' or 'heated,' Ref. (Ibid, p. IX)

It can be logically concluded that the people inhabiting the earth after the flood were of African/Edenic descent. The only time the scriptures mention a change of color pigmentation on a permanent basis is written in 2 Kings 5:15-27.

When famine swept the land of Canaan, Joseph's brothers went into Egypt seeking grain. They saw Joseph but they did not recognize him, but he knew them. The Canaanites and early Israelites were black, as well as Egyptians to *engage in 'corrective historiography' attest to the fact that it is no longer enough to limit the discussion to "black theology' or even African theology; instead, Africa, her people, nations, and cultures, must be acknowledged as making primary, direct contributions to the development of Christianity. The purpose of the Original African Heritage Study Bible is to interpret the Bible as it relates specifically to persons of African descent and thereby to foster an appreciation of the multiculturalism inherent in the Bible.*

We believe it's important to stress that our research is not presented from a racist viewpoint of racial pluralism and inclusiveness, seeking to bring forth the truth from a story which has had many dubious interpretations...

Recently, in American and in Africa, there has developed a proliferation of books and pamphlets which represent a resurgence of what may be called Afrocentric approaches to the Bible...Ref. (Ibid p. VIII)

The *'curse of Ham'* is a post-biblical myth. In Gen. 9:18-29, Ham is not the recipient of a curse. The text explicitly says, 'Let *Canaan* be cursed.' Furthermore, Ham does not mean 'black' in Hebrew, it translates literally as *'hot' or 'heated.'* Ref. (Ibid, p. IX). It can be logically concluded that the people inhabiting the earth after the flood were of African/Edenic descent. The only time the scriptures mention a change of color pigmentation on a permanent basis is written in 2 Kings 5:15-27.

When famine swept the land of Canaan, Joseph's brothers went into Egypt seeking grain. They saw Joseph but they did not recognize him, but he knew them. *The Canaanites and early Israelites were black, as well as the Egyptians. Joseph looked just as the Egyptians.* This passage validates the skin color of not only the Egyptians but also the *African/Edenic Israelites*. There is little doubt of the skin texture of the Shulamite woman who speaks in Song of Songs 1:5. This woman is known to have been the Queen of Sheba, also known as Bilquis, and Jesus called her Queen of the South. The land of Sheba was a colony of Ethiopians who settled in Arabia from Ethiopia. The Queen ruled both territories. Goliath was a Philistine and one of the original inhabitants of Canaan. The Philistines were black descendants of Cush.

There is no biblical story any more fascinating than that of these two personalities. Delilah was a Philistine woman whose people were always at odds with the Israelites. Her beauty, as with all of the Canaanite women, was tantalizing to Samson. The Israelites were told time after time by the Lord God of Israel to leave Canaanite women alone. Samson himself was a dark-skinned person from the tribe of Dan whose present descendants live in modern-day Ethiopia, a remnant of the original Jews. The King James translators referred to his hair as being in locks, but the closest translation would have been 'plaits', which was an ancient African custom. Ref. (The Original African Heritage Study Bible p. 47).

God's Plan for the Sons of Ham

The following paragraphs are legendary, but contain some truth:

Queen Makeda (the Queen of Sheba) stayed in Jerusalem for six months, during which time her union with King Solomon produced Menelik I, who was born while she journeyed back to Ethiopia. There she condemned the sun god worship as well other types of worship and introduced to her people the worship of the True God of King Solomon of Israel. She made history as a woman responsible for a mass reformation in the history of Ethiopia, where the worship of the One True God was officially established. In later years when her son, Menelik I, visited his father, King Soloman, and returned to Ethiopia, as well as other natives, trace their descent from the people who accompanied Menelik to Ethiopia.

The Kebra Negast states that when Menelik I. visited his father King Solomon in Jerusalem, Menelik expressed his desire to take to his country the Ark of the Covenant, which is the Tables of the Law that God had given to Moses that had journeyed through the ages with the children of Israel until they acquired kings to rule over them. Now this Ark rested in the possession of King Solomon, and Zadok, the high priest, chief among the priests of Israel, who ministered before the Ark. Whenever the priests made their supplications to God, provided it was in accordance with the will of

God, the Ark would rise from where it lay. It was the will of God that the Ark be transferred to Ethiopia. Azarias, son of Zadok, and all the men if Israel who were to accompany Menelik to Ethiopia planned to take the Ark by hiring a carpenter to make a duplicate of it. When it was completed, the angel of the Lord appeared to Azarias and instructed him on how he and his brethren should go about taking the Ark.

They were to make sacrifices for the atonement of their sins; then the priests were to bring into the temple the replica made by the carpenters. An angel of the Lord would open the door of the House of the Lord for them, at which point they were to take the Ark of the Covenant. Everything was accomplished, the real Ark was taken with the aid of the angel of the Lord, and they put the duplicate in its place.

Although the priest Azarias and other priests feared to take the Ark, they were encouraged by the angel's words: 'Fear not. Take courage. Thou must call Elmeas and Abyssa, the brothers, and Meukri. Thou shall bring them the little boards of wood. I shall open for thee the doors of the House of the Lord. Thou shalt take the Tables of the Law, without fear, without sorrow, without risk of being punished. I have been appointed by God to abide near them. I shall be thy guide while thou goest to remove them.'

And so it was done, Menelik and Azarias and all the firstborn of Israel packed and journeyed in a miraculously short time to Ethiopia, upon seeing this, Queen Makeda was so overjoyed that she prostrated herself, glorifying the Almighty God, and there occurred in Ethiopia a great celebration. Upon this great and memorable occasion of the arrival of the Ark of the Covenant in Ethiopia, perhaps the greatest occurrence in ancient Ethiopian church history, the queen of Sheba addressed her subjects closing with the following command: "Love ye what is right is righteousness and falsehood is the head of iniquity. And ye shall not use fraud and oppression among yourselves, for God dwelleth with you and the habitation of His Glory is among you: for you have become members of His household. And from this time onward cease ye to observe your former customs, namely making auguries from birds, and from signs and from magic. And if after this day there be found any man who observed all his former customs, his house shall be plundered and he his wife and his children shall be condemned.'

The worship of God was then officially established, and she abdicated the throne and gave it to her son, Menelik I, who was crowned King of Kings. Thus began in Ethiopia the Solomonian dynasty of kings that lasted to the twentieth century. It should be noted, however, that the Solomonic kingdom in Ethiopia should not be considered as the root of The Ethiopian kingdom but as an additional blessing from God, for the country had been ruled by kings for thousands of years before Menelik I came to the throne. The removal of the Ark of the Covenant was truly a historic event which is venerated greatly by Ethiopians. Today the Ark of the Covenant of God lies in the St. Mary of Zion Church in the sacred city of Axum, which is the birthplace of the Ethiopian civiliza-tion and center for Christian Worship.

Today Axum is a town in the province of Tigre, where the glories of the past remain. The 67-foot-high obelisk, carved from sold granite, with its massive pillars, and the Taka Mariam Palace, are evidence of Axum's ancient and glorious past. The spirit of the queen of Sheba's existence in ancient Axum seems to linger in traditions of the Old Testament. A priest still performs services before the Ark in modern Ethiopia. Ref. (Unknown)

History tells us that horrendous lies began to be told about Blacks as early as the late 1700's, particularly coming out of Gottingen University in Germany. Professor Blumenbach first postulated the superiority of Caucasians over blacks and others. (Nile Valley Contributions to Civ., p. 19). These lies have continued to be told until today. As late as 1974 there was an important symposium held in Cairo, Egypt. It was given by UNESCO. Some of the greatest anthropologists from around the world came. Many came from Europe and from America, Caucasian men of great learning. There were twenty altogether. Eighteen were from Europe and America, only two were from Africa. Many lies had been told up to that time. They were even trying to say that Egyptians and Ethiopians were not black Africans. In fact, they were saying that these Africans were dark-skinned Europeans! One of the African anthropologists, Dr. Cheikh Anta Diop, proved without a doubt, through a melanin test on the skin of Egyptians mummies, that Egyptians were indeed Negroid people! *(Nile Valley Contrib. to Civ., p. 19).*

When the British followed Napoleon into Egypt and stole much of what his scholars had gathered there in the 1800s, the study of Egypt reached the heights of greatness. We find from history that once the Europeans rediscovered the greatness of Egypt, their scholars began to deny the color of the Egyptians.

Prior to this time, even up through the times of Homer and Herodotus, Egypt's greatness and the dark-skinned color of its people were known. Herodotus who was called the Father of History, and Homer, who was one of the great poets of Greece, did not have racial prejudices based on color as men have today. We need to understand that this **color thing** only became a problem after African slavery had become a **big business** in the known world. Keep this in mind, for if you understand this, you will understand their typing to justify marketing human flesh and slavery, and demeaning people of black skins.

History tells us that somewhere between eighty to one hundred million black people were taken out of Africa. Only a third of them made it to the New World to become slaves; the rest died on the arduous journeys across the Atlantic. We are taking time to explain to you how racial prejudice came to be based on color, where it had not been a problem in ancient times.

Let us also admit that in ancient times when black people ruled the world, that is Egypt and Ethiopia, it is said that the Ethiopian empire stretched as far east as India and China. When Egypt was in power her influence extended as far as eastern Europe and they brought captives out of Russia and Poland, and made them slaves in Egypt *(Your History* by J.A. Rogers).

God's Plan for the Sons of Ham

CHAPTER SEVEN
GOD FAVORS HAM FIRST

Let me, at this point, make one of the major statements of this book. God, even the Creator God, Jehovah, Creator of the heavens and earth, is a **just** God! We will find written in the 18th chapter of Genesis verse 25, the following statement:

> *"Shall not the judge of all the earth do right?"*

This God purposed and ordained in His original plan that the offspring of the three sons on Noah, Shem, Ham and Japheth, each would have their turn at ruling the world. This God believes in equality and fairness!

Let us get back to the point we were making concerning ancient times. We must understand that the Canaanites were black people. Canaan was the fourth son of Ham. Ham means *heat, hot, or sunburnt.* He was clearly a dark-skinned or black man. The Bible enables us to see that God allowed the first rulers of the known world to be the sons of Ham. We find that their rule lasted around three thousand years.

Then we will find in history that God gave Israel a king in the person of Saul. Afterwards David ruled as king, and then Solomon. Israel learned about kings from the Hamitic people, that is, the Canaanite people whom God sent them among to drive them from their delightsome land or pleasant land known as Canaan. God purposed to give that land to Israel as an inheritance, because of the Canaanites' wickedness, pride, idolatry and lewdness. God allowed the sons of **Shem** to rule the known world for some seven hundred years. They included the Israelites, the Assyrians, the Babylonians and the Medo-Persians, He allowed the sons of **Japheth** (Europeans) to begin to rule the world through the Greeks. They began to rule in the year 326 B.C. (Daniel 8:21). They have ruled the world up until this present time, nearly two thousand, two hundred year.

The point we are attempting to make is that early on, in the times of Homer and Herodotus, which is late really, racial prejudice based on color was unknown. I want you to know that Nimrod lived some three thousand years before Christ. His Kingdom was established way back then. Nubians, Egyptians and Ethiopians can be traced to that period of time when they began to rule the known world. A headline in the New York Times for March 1, 1979 was: **Ancient Nubian Artifacts Yield Evidence of Earliest Monarchy.**

The Nubians made tremendous discoveries in the heavenly bodies, and great discoveries on the earth. They devised and brought forth such, academic fields as chemistry, physics and mathematics. They became great architects and built the pyramids; which men have not fully understood until this day. We have come to understand that the pyramids were not burial places for the great pharaohs, but were **astronomical observatories!** It was from these observation towers that the Egyptians, Ethiopians and the Nubians were able to observe the heavenly bodies. They built the pyramids and lined them up to the north pole and the south pole. They were used for scientific purposes of a very high order. These men were geniuses. I call these early ancient people **super-geniuses!**

In order to understand how some of the ancient people felt about these beautiful black people, I will refer to Anthony Browder's book on *The Nile Valley Contributions to Civilization.* Then I will also quote from the introduction of *The Original African Heritage Study Bible* where some quotes are taken from some great minds.

In Anthony Browder's book *The Nile Valley Contributions to Civilization,* page 137, he writes:

The suggestion that the history of ancient Egypt would be rewritten to support a racist ideology, is more than a notion. In the eighteenth century a Frenchmen by the name of Count Constantine de Volney (1757-1820) wrote a wonderful history book titled The Ruin of Empires, which describes his journeys in Egypt between 1783 and 1785. This book became a best seller in France and demand for it was so great that an English version was printed in an'American edition.' The American edition became available in the mid 1790's.

Volney's descriptions of the ancient monuments were fair and objective. He described the appearance of the Sphinx as typically Negro in all of its features. To some, Volney's descriptions were too accurate, and they had to be modified. For example, British editors decided to omit several lines of the text from pages 15, 16 and 17 in the American edition of Ruins of Empires. One specific quotation describes the ancient kingdoms of Ethiopia and Egyptian city of Thebes. Another edited statement which describes the people of Kemet reads: "There are a people now forgotten, who discovered while others were yet barbarians, the elements of art and sciences. A race of men, now ejected from society for their sable skin and frizzled hair, founded on the study of laws of nature and those civil and religious systems which still govern the universe."

Volney discovered this glaring omission only after he had mastered the English language, and he forbade the future sale of his works until such time that it could be published in its entirety. This act of censorship was certainly not an isolated incident. It was representative of a clear and consistent pattern of covering up and denying African historical accomplishments. The gross misrepresentation of Nile Valley history has been referred to us as a 'stolen legacy,' and have been perpetrated by many, learned scholars for hundreds of years.

Two millennia prior to Volney's travels to the Nile Valley, other Europeans wrote about their experiences and observations. Like Volney, these travelers described people of color whom fifteenth Century Europeans would later enslave and classify as, Negroes. As early as the eighth century B.C.E. Homer in the Iliad, stated that Zeus and all the gods of Greece traveled to Africa, to feast with Ethiopia's faultness men. Four hundred years later the historian Herodotus remarked: 'Almost all the names of the gods came into Greece from Egypt. My inquiries prove that they were all derived from a foreign source, and my opinion is that Egypt furnished the greater number. The Egyptians were the first to introduce solemn assemblies, possessions, and litanies to the gods, all of which the Greeks were taught to use. It seems to me a sufficient proof of this is that in Egypt these practices had to have been established from remote antiquity, while in Greece they are only recently known,'... Herodotus also described the Egyptians as 'black-skinned' and having 'wooly hair'.

Four hundred years after the visit of Herodotus to Africa, a Sicilian writer name Diodorus recorded his observations of the Nile Valley: "The Ethiopians say that the Egyptians were one of their colonies which was brought into Egypt by Osiris. They add that from them as their authors and ancestors, the Egyptians get most of their laws. It is from them that Egyptians have learned to honor kings as gods and bury them with such pomp; sculpture and writing were invented by the Ethiopians."

Let us now draw a few quotes from the introduction to the African Heritage Study Bible. On page 109, under the heading of "Africa's Service to the World," we read:

There has been an unbroken line of communication between the west coast of Africa, through the Sudan, and through the so-called Great Desert and Asia, from the time when portions of the descendants of Ham, in remote ages, began their migration westward and saw the Atlantic Ocean. Africa is no vast island, separated by an immense ocean from other portions of the globe, cut off through the ages from men who have made and influenced the destinies of mankind. She had long been closely connected, both as source and nourisher, with some of the most potent influences which have affected for good the history of the world. The people of Asia and the people of Africa have been in constant intercourse. No violent social or political disruption has ever broken through this communication. No chasm caused by war has suspended intercourse. On the contrary, the greatest religious reforms the world has ever seen: Jewish, Christian, Muslim originated in Africa/Asia, and obtained consolidation in Africa. As in the days of Abraham and Moses, of Herodotus and Homer, so today, there is a constantly accessible highway from Asia to the heart of the Sudan. Africans are continually going to and fro between the Atlantic Ocean and the Red Sea. Africans were not unknown, therefore, to the writers of the Bible. Their peculiarities of complexion and hair were as well known to the ancient Greeks and Hebrews, as they are to the American people today. When they spoke of the Ethiopians, they meant the ancestors of the black-skinned and wooly-haired people who, for two hundred fifty years, have been known as laborers on the plantations of the South. It is to these people, and to their country, that the Psalmist refers, (68:31) Ethiopia shall soon stretch out her hands unto God. The word in the original, which has been translated 'soon'; Ethiopia shall suddenly stretch out her hands unto God, is the most recent rendering."

God's Plan for the Sons of Ham

Another peculiarity that the author points out that has been observed in the people of Ham, the African, Afro-Asiatic and Afro-Edenic people, is that they have consistently, throughout their history held to the view of a Great Creator, the One who created the heavens, earth, sun, moon and stars. They believe in Him as the:

'Almighty personal Agent, who is their own Maker and Sovereign, and they render to Him such worship as their untutored intellects can conceive...'

And this peculiarity of Africa is not a thing known only in modern times. The ancients recognized these qualities and loved to descant upon them. They seemed to regard the fear and love of God as a peculiar gift of the darker races. In the version of the Chaldean Genesis: 'The Word of the Lord will never fail in the mouth of the dark races whom He has made!' Homer and Herodotus have written immortal eulogies of the race. Homer speaks of them as the blameless Ethiopians' and tells us that it was the Ethiopians alone among mortals whom the gods selected (and they are talking about Greek gods) as a people fit to be lifted to the social level of the Olympian divinities. Every year, the poet says, the whole celestial circle left the summits of the Olympus and betook themselves, for their holidays, to Ethiopia where in the enjoyment of Ethiopian hospitality, they sojourned twelve days.
"This is a quote from that day:

*The Sire of gods and all the ethereal train
On the warm limits of the farthest main
Now mix with mortals, nor disdain to grace
Feasts of Ethiopia's blameless race;
Twelve days the Powers indulge the genial rite,
Returning with the twelfth revolving night.'*

I say again, without fear of contradiction that the early people of Ham, the people of color, the black people, were like a super-race of people. They were like super-geniuses, when we are honest. Through the diggings of archaeologist, especially with the discovery of the Rosetta Stone toward the end of the 1800's, scholars have been able to determine that these ancient dark-skinned people, black people and sons of Ham did indeed lay the foundation upon which all of western civilization and all the civilized people of the world have built.

I am so glad that I did not write this. I discovered this is secular writings, in writings by scholars who are not necessarily men of the cloth or men of the Bible; but I have also discovered some of this in the Bible itself!

We have tried to point out that the ancient, dark-skinned, Black people of Afro-Edenic origins, the people who originally inhabited what we know as Africa, and today is known as the Middle East, were people upon whom God showered great favor. They were people whom God treated like the **firstborn** of Noah rather than the second born. Shem was the firstborn of Noah. God chose out of his seed through Abraham, to establish a covenant that would lead to a covenant of redemption in the Lord Jesus Christ, that Seed through whom all the families of the earth would be blessed!

CHAPTER EIGHT
GOD'S PLAN AND HAM'S FALL

We will now endeavor to show, by the Word of the Lord, that it was the Maker's plan, the plan of the God and Father or our Lord Jesus Christ, to cause a mixing of the seed of **Shem** (through David, Judah, Joseph and Abraham) with the seed of **Ham**, so that the great Seed produced, finally would be the Lord Jesus Christ, the Savior of the world! Jesus Christ was of the House of Judah, and in Him flowed the blood of African (or Hamitic) people.

We purpose to show through this writing that it was a part of God's plan, that some of the people out of Ham should be connected with and mixed with some of the people of Shem, and that we, as a people, **together**, would bring great blessings to the world!

As we continue with our discussion of the Afro-Asiatic man, the Afro-Edenic man, the dark-skinned man, the sable-skinned man, the Hamitic man, we want to point out that we have already looked at this man in secular history, from the writings of such men as Homer and Herodotus, etc. We have seen their estimation of these sable-skinned or dark-skinned people, who were super-geniuses in the earth, and who laid the foundations of what we now know as civilization, especially Western civilization.

Let us now go to the Holy Scriptures and get their testimony concerning this dark-skinned man, this Hamitic man, into whom God chose to pour His wisdom, so much so, that he was almost like God. He was so God-like, as a result of his being so greatly imbued with the wisdom of God, that he became exalted by his own beauty. As a result, this man became so lifted up God had to bring him down.

What I find in scripture are passages that are set over against the Hamitic man's downfall and provide the reasons for it. I questioned the Lord for several weeks and, while flying to Uganda in May, 1994, I asked, "Lord if black people were so great early in civilization, why have we suffered so tremendously throughout the history of humankind and especially in the past two hundred and fifty to three hundred years"?

In slavery, we were counted as less than nothing; we were counted as brute beasts. Why has it been recorded that some of our white American leaders, both political and religious have said, "Let us shut out all forms of light from the minds of these people. Let them be as brute beasts. Don't let them read!"

Some secular black scholars have said that history runs in cycles. In one cycle, one group is on top, and in another cycle, the top group sinks to the bottom, and the bottom group rises to the top. Such reasoning does not acknowledge the universal law of cause and effect. This law says "for every action, there is an equal and opposite reaction. "So, the first answer is inadequate and therefore unacceptable.

Another position taken by some Black biblical scholars is that the Black man's awful sufferings may be likened to the sufferings of Job. Job happens to be from the tribe of Esau (or so it is alleged by some), and since Esau married both Ishmaelite and Hittite (Canaanite) wives. Then his offspring were strongly Hamitic or Black. Job's name means one who is persecuted; and in all of his sufferings he was patient and did not charge God for his problems and troubles. They believe that black people in human history have done likewise.

We believe the severe suffering of the black man in history is based on his violation of two biblical principles. These principles are found in the gospels. The first one found in Luke 12:47-48 says:

> *"And that servant, which knew his lord's will, and prepared not himself, neither did according to his will, shall be beaten with many stripes. But he that knew not, and did commit things worthy of stripes, shall be beaten with few stripes. For unto whomever much is given, of him shall much be required: and to whom men have committed much, of him will they ask the more."*

The sons of Ham, whom God treated as firstborn, are the ones who received God's greatest strength, blessings and wisdom to be the first world rulers and leaders. They knew the will of God. Noah, who was a righteous man who walked with God, knew the will of God and taught it to his sons. Paul wrote:

> *"Because that, when they knew God, they glorified him not as God...but became vain in their imaginations, and their foolish heart was darkened. Professing themselves to be wise they became fools."*
> (Romans 1:21-22)

We believe the passages above refer to the Tower of Babel whose construction was headed up by Nimrod, the builder. Micah 5:6 calls Assyria "the land of Nimrod." Genesis 10:10-11 says:

> *"And the beginning of his (Nimrod's) kingdom was*

Babel…in the land of Shinar…from that land he went to Assyria and built Ninevah."

The second very serious principle in God's word which the early Hamitic leaders violated is found in Matthew 23:12, which says:

"Whosoever shall exalt himself shall be abased."

Another applicable passage relative to the sons of Ham's great sins against God are found in Exodus 20:2-5. There God said:

"I am the Lord your God…You shall have no other gods before me! You shall not make for yourself a carved image…You shall not bow down to them nor sever them." NKJV

Again, Paul wrote:

"And (they) changed the glory of the incorruptible God into an image made like unto corruptible man…. Who changed the truth of God into a lie, and worshipped and served the creature more than the Creator…" (Romans 1:23, 25)

It is well documented in history and in the Bible that God's first world leaders and rulers, the sons of Ham, initiated the practice of emperor or pharaoh worship. It began with men worshipping Nimrod the *"mighty one,"* and then worshipping great Black kings and pharaohs (Ezekiel 28: 1-9, Isaiah 19:1-3, 11-12). Ham's offspring led in the practice of idolatry at the Tower of Babel, the practice of homosexuality at Sodom and Gomorrah, and initiated human sacrifice in Canaan (Genesis 19).

When the flesh, or the selfish base drive of mankind is left unchecked and unfiltered, then all types of sinful mindsets, behaviors and possibilities are unleashed by humans, regardless of race. Since many of the descendants of Ham allowed themselves to both seek to replace the Lord God in their thinking and acting, without any respect or Repentance, God fulfilled His Word of discipline to bring them down to the positon of being dominated by others. The good news is that this divine discipline is not forever and I will discuss the comeback of the Sons of Ham in future chapters.

CHAPTER NINE
THE UNFOLDING OF GOD'S PLAN

Let us began our journey in the Scriptures in the eighth number of the book of Psalms. The writer is believed to be King David, the sweet Psalmist of Israel. In verse 3, of this Psalm, it says:

> "When I consider thy heavens, the work of thy fingers (talking about God Almighty) the moon and the stars, which thou hast ordained: What is man, that thou are mindful of him? And the son of man, that thou visitest him? For thou hast made him a little lower than the angels."

In the original, it says, *"You have made him a little lower than Elohim."* Elohim is God's name that He used in reference to the creation in Genesis. It reads:

> *"In the beginning God created the heavens and the earth, and God said, let there be, and it was..."*

In other words, this is God's name that speaks of Him as the **Almighty** Creator. Here it says, *"You have made him a little lower than Elohim."* (You have made man a little lower than the Creator, Almighty God himself!) *"You have crowned him with glory and honor"* (verse 6). *"You have made him to have dominion over the works of your hands; you have put all things under his feet."*

As we move through the history of the Bible, we see the seed of Shem and Ham being co-mingled in marriage and in concubinage, etc. We find that not only did Abram go into Hagar, (the Egyptian) at his wife Sarai's request, and have a son by her (when Abram had no children and Sarai was barren), we find that later, after the death of Sarah, that Abraham married a black woman by the name of Keturah, and that she gave Abraham six sons, one of whom was Midian.

I want you to stop and consider that David, the sweet Psalmist of Israel, was of the House of Judah. We find in Genesis chapter 28 that Judah married a Canaanite woman, the daughter of Shuah. Judah, whose name means *praise*, inadvertently had a set of twins by his daughter-in-law, whose name was Tamar, also a Canaanite.

Not only did Judah go into the land of Canaan and

select a black wife, and not only did Abraham marry a Hamitic wife after the death of his beloved Sarah, but Abraham himself was a dark-skinned man.

When Moses fled from the land of Egypt after he had killed an Egyptian man, he fled into the desert, into the wilderness as it were. He found himself in a land called Midian. The Midianites were the offspring of Abraham and Keturah. They were definitely black people. Please refer to the book of numbers, chapter twelve and verse one for confirmation of my statement above.

After Moses led the children of Israel out of Egyptian bondage, they were encamped around Sinai, receiving instructions from the Lord, through His servant. Moses had taken Zipporah as his wife, one of the daughters of Jethro, a Midianite priest, during his forty-year sojourn in the land of Midian.

Isn't it strange that this Midianite priest was able to train Moses in the ways of the God of Abraham, Isaac and Jacob? How is that? Because he was an offspring of Abraham, and God had boasted about Abraham in the 18th chapter of Genesis saying, *"I know him, I know he will train his children in the way of the Lord."* Abraham had taken it upon himself to train his six sons (by his black wife Keturah) in the ways of the Lord, in the ways of Jehovah. These sons trained their sons on down the line. Now Jethro, an offspring of Abraham and Keturah, a black man, trained his own son-in-law. For forty years he was Moses' mentor in the ways of Jehovah. He prepared him for his burning bush experience that we read about in the Old Testament (Exodus 3).

Now Moses, after having that experience, went back to Egypt and brought the children of Israel out by the mighty hand of God. Having crossed the Red Sea, they are now encamped around Mt. Sinai. Jethro brought Moses' wife Zipporah, and their two sons to Moses there at the encampment. Moses went and bowed down and showed reverence to his mentor of forty years, this black man named Jethro. Moses was also a dark-skinned man, because the Egyptians were dark-skinned people, as the testimony of Herodotus, Homer and others bear witness from secular records. They were dark-skinned people with wooly hair.

Moses was able to pass as one of them growing up in the courts of Pharaoh. You know the story. He was drawn out of the river, at a time when Pharaoh was slaughtering Hebrew baby boys in Egypt, in order to decrease their numbers in population. Moses was hidden in a little boat of bulrushes and was found by the Pharaoh's daughter, and was raised in the courts of Pharaoh as the grandson of Pharaoh. Moses looked like the Egyptians; he had to be a dark-skinned man in order to be accepted as one of them.

Nevertheless, Moses and Zipporah were married, and in the book of Numbers 12:1 we find Aaron and Miriam rising up and complaining against the fact that he had married an Ethiopian or Cushite (black) woman. The word *Ethiopia,* comes from the Greek word *Ethiopes,* which means *burnt-face people.*

Moses had married this woman, and their argument against him was not so much because Moses was white or light skinned, but because she was of a different *ethnic* group than the Isralites (Hebrews).

Isn't it interesting that Jethro, Moses' father in law, was able to lead Aaron and the rest of the priesthood in the offering of sacrifices to the God of Abraham, Isaac and Jacob? He had been trained and taught in this by his forefathers, going back to Abraham (Exodus 18:12; Genesis 18:19).

David was of the house of Judah. Judah married a black, Canaanite wife and Judah fathered a set of twins through his Canaanite daughter-in-law, Tamar. We read about this in the 38th chapter of Genesis, where the account is described as this. After Judah's wife died, he was evidently accustomed to finding harlots along the road, with whom he would lie in order to satisfy his sexual needs. On this occasion, as he went in and lay with this supposed harlot, he did not know that it was his daughter-in-law!

Let us look into the Gospel of St. Matthew, chapter one. Here is the genealogy of Jesus Christ, showing David to be one of his forefathers. Beginning at verse one we read:

"The book of the genealogy of Jesus Christ, the son of

David, the son of Abraham. Abraham begat Isaac; and Isaac begat Jacob; and Jacob; begat Judas; and his brethren; And Judas begat Phares and Zara of Thamar (remember who Tamar is?) and Phares begat Esrom; and Esrom begat Aram; and Aram begat Aminadab; and Aminadab begat Naasson; and Naasson begat Salmon."

Who was Salmon? We will let our minds go back to the story (in the book of Joshua) of the children of Israel going into conquer and to take the land of Canaan. The Canaanites were dispossessed of their inheritance, and their land went to the children of Israel. The reason the Canaanites were dispossessed was because of their gross wickedness. Remember they were brilliant people. (We will read about a Canaanite king in the 28th chapter of Ezekiel). They were driven out of the land, but not all of them were driven out. Of those who were, some went into the southernmost parts of Africa, central Africa, and some were scattered throughout the world. This is the reason European explorers found blacks in Central and South America when they went into Mexico and the Caribbean. They found African types of people there. How did they get there? Evidently, they came by boat or they went over land. *(Nile Valley Contributions to Civ.* p.p. 209-212). That is another story in itself.

We find that Salmon begat Boaz by Rahab. Do you remember Rahab? She was the black, Canaanite harlot who hid the two spies when the twelve spies went into the land of Canaan to spy out the land. Therefore, her household was shown favor and was spared when the children of Israel went in and took Jericho, (Joshua 2:12-19 and 6:22-23). Rahab was not only spared, but she married a Jewish man, one from the tribe of Judah whose name was **Salmon**. Salmon and Rahab produced Boaz. Boaz begat Obed by Ruth, who a Moabitess, whose story is in the book of Ruth. Boaz was a dark-skinned man, coming from Rahab his black mother and from Salmon who was from the tribe of Judah, a dark-skinned tribe, by virtue of Judah's intermarriage with a black Canaanite woman, and his subsequent tryst with his daughter-in-law, Tamar.

King David begat Solomon by her who had been the wife of Uriah, who was none other than Bathsheba, a black Hittite, Canaanite woman. This beautiful woman became the mother of Solomon by David. Solomon was black (Song of Solomon 1:5-6), and Solomon begat Rehoboam and Rehoboam begat Abia, and Abia begat Asa. The story continues and concludes with Jesus Christ. Not only did David have rich Hamitic, Afro-Asiatic blood running through his veins, so also did our precious Lord Jesus Christ!

Let's summarize what we have learned thus far. We see throughout the Old Testament that major patriarchs such as Abraham, Judah, Moses, Jethro, Boaz and King David, who are all from the posterity of Shem, intermarried with the daughters from the progeny of Ham. There seems to be quite a bit of the descendants of Shem spending time in the tents of Ham, which counteracts the curse of Noah in Genesis 9:27, "May God enlarge (the land of) Japheth, and let him dwell in the tents of Shem; and let Canaan be his servant."

This should awaken many to the fact that whomever the Lord blesses, no man can curse! All people of color hold a special place in the heart of the Lord, and He wants all human beings to respect one another as His handiwork and master creation.

CHAPTER TEN
THE GREATNESS AND DOWNFALL OF HAM'S SONS

Let us move on to the 28th chapter of Ezekiel. Here we find God speaking to the King of Tyre. What was Tyre? Tyre was a Sidonian city. Who were the Sidonians? They were from Sidon, the firstborn son of Canaan (Genesis 10:15). In history, we find the Sidonians to have been called the Phoenicians (Acts 15:3). This is what the Greeks called them.

When I studied history in Junior high school or college. I never knew that the Phoenicians were black people. I want to interject here that the Phoenicians had a part in inventing a portion of the alphabet. The alphabet began in ancient Nubia and went from there to Kemet or ancient Nubia and went from there to Kemet or ancient

Egypt. It was then improved upon by the Phoenicians or the Sidonians, and then by the Greeks and Romans.

The Phoenicians also originated metal coins, and were among the earliest great shipbuilders. They sailed the seven seas, and were great traders in merchandise, for they had beautiful things to bring out of Canaan, which was a part of Africa. It was that pleasant land, that delightsome land that was later called Palestine. Out of Sidon came beautiful jewels and topaz, gold, rich spices and etc. You can read about it in 1 Kings 5:1-18, when King Hiram came to visit Solomon and brought all these riches. He also brought great carvers, stone-cutters, cedars of Lebanon, and all the materials and people necessary to do a great work in assisting in the building of the Temple of Solomon.

We see then, that the King of Tyrus was Canaanite, a black king out of Canaan, the fourth son of Ham. Ezekiel wrote:

> *"Son of man, say unto the prince of Tyrus, thus saith the Lord God, because thine heart is lifted up, and thou hast said, I am a god."*

I have a sneaking suspicion that the King of Tyrus said that he was a "god" because of his great wisdom! I pause here to say that the one thing God had against Egypt was that, due to their great wisdom and all the tremendous things their genius enabled them to produce, they began to worship their pharaohs as gods. They saw the sun in the sky as their chief god. They begin to worship pharaoh as the son of Ra or the son of that god.

This was also a big problem for Nimrod, because he was called a Gibbor (in Hebrew) or a mighty one. He was a man of great renown, a man who built cities and kingdoms, who was also a great archer and a great warrior. Because of Nimrod's great reputation people began to make statuettes of him as the child of the Madonna. They worshipped him, which the true God has always been against. God said to the children of Israel in the 20th chapter of Exodus, as they came out of Egypt, and were encamped around Sinai:

> *"Thou shall have no gods before me. I am the LORD, thy God that brought thee out of Egypt on eagles' wings. Thou shalt make no graven image of anything on the earth, in the sea, beneath the sea or any such thing."* (Exodus 20:2-4)

So, the Lord says to the King of Tyre:

> *Because your heart is lifted up and you say I am a god, I sit in the seat of God in the midst of the seas, yet you are a man and not a god…You shall die the death of the slain in the midst of the seas.*
> (Ezekiel 28:2, 8 NKJV)

Let us pause here and say that this kind of rebuke was germane to black-skinned and dark-skinned men of great renown in ancient times. We might say that God is speaking generically to The Black man, who He treated as the firstborn of Noah, one who most closely resembled his original man, Adam; one who failed Him.

The latter portion of verse two of the 28th chapter of Ezekiel says:

"Yet you are a man and not a god, you set your heart as the heart of God."

You set it as though you have a mind almost like God himself! Ezekiel 28:3 says:

"Behold you are wiser than Daniel!"

Let us turn to the 9th chapter of the book of Daniel, verse 22, to see what the Lord has to say to Daniel there, through the angel Gabriel. In the book of Daniel, chapter four, king Nebuchadnezzar had a great dream that troubled him. The king called for Daniel, after his own soothsayers, magicians and wise men could not interpret the dream. Verse 8 says:

But at last Daniel came before me, whose name was Belteshazzar, according to the name of my god and in him is the spirit of the holy gods, and I told the dream before him saying, "Belteshazzar, chief of the magicians, because I know what the spirit of the holy gods is in you and no secret troubles you, explain to me the vision that I have seen and its interpretation.' NKJV

After Nebuchadnezzar explained the vision to Daniel, Daniel began to give him the interpretation. Verse 18, Chapter 4, says:

> *"This dream I king Nebuchadnezzar have seen. Now thou, O Belteshazzar, declare unto me the interpretation since all the wise men of my kingdom are not able to make known into me the interpretation but you are able, for the spirit of the holy gods is in you."*

In chapter nine of Daniel, after Daniel has prayed and fasted, confessed his sins and the sins of Israel his people unto God, while he was yet speaking, Gabriel the angel, whom he had seen in a vision at the beginning, began to speak to him. Verse 22 says:

> *"And he informed me, and talked with me, and said, 'Daniel, I am now come forth to give you skill to understand. At the beginning of your supplications the command went out, and I am come to tell you; for you are greatly beloved, therefore consider the matter*

and understand the vision." (NKJV)

Daniel was given skill to understand the secret things of God that were shared in vision form. With all this great wisdom, and even having an excellent spirit, as it is said in the 28th chapter verse three of Ezekiel to the king of Tyre:

> *"Behold you are wiser than Daniel! There are no secrets that can be hidden from you, with your wisdom and with your understanding you have gained riches for yourself. You gathered gold and silver into your treasures and by your great wisdom in trade you have increased your riches and your heart is lifted up because of your riches."* (NKJV)

This is one of the reasons God brought down the highly exalted, super-genius, generic Black man, the Afro-Asiatic man, who sprang from Africa. God gave him the most and the best of everything at the beginning. He became lifted up because of the riches his great wisdom had gained him. Verse six says:

> *Therefore because you have set your heart as the heart of a god, behold, I will bring strangers against you, the most terrible of the nations, and they will draw their sword against the beauty of your wisdom, and defile your splendor. They shall throw you down into*

the pit.

Verse 9 says:

"Will you still say to him that slays you, I am a god? But you shall be a man and not a god in the hands that slays you. You shall die the death of the uncircumcised by the hands of aliens, for I have spoken it says the Lord God." (NKJV)

Verse 11 says:

"Moreover the word of the Lord came unto me saying (that is to Ezekiel), Son of man, take up a lamentation of the king of Tyrus and say to him, 'Thus says the Lord God, you were the seal of perfection, full of wisdom and perfect in beauty.'"

In other words, you were the absolute sum. You were the last word when it came to perfection because you were full of wisdom and perfect in beauty. Verse 13 says:

"You were in Eden (that delightsome land, that pleasant land) the garden of God (which was none other than Africa, as we told you from the beginning). Every precious stone was your covering."

Africa is known to be the continent richest in minerals,

precious stones and in gold.

> "Every precious stone was our covering, sardius, diamond, beryl, onyx and the jasper."

Let us read from Genesis 2:11-12:

> "The name of the first river is Pison, it is the one that skirts the whole land of Havilah (as we have told you Havilah was one of the sons of Cush, the black man, the eldest son of Ham) where there is gold. And the gold of that land is good. Bdellium and the onyx stone are there." (NKJV)

Clearly this is Africa, we don't need to belabor the point! The word of the Lord in Ezekiel 28:13 says:

> "You were in Eden the garden of God, every precious stone was your covering: the sardius, topaz and diamond, beryl, onyx and jasper, sapphire, turquoise, emerald and gold." (NKJV)

We are clearly talking about the same place that we read about in the second chapter of Genesis! Understand that God is speaking generically to the black man whom He exalted highly in the early days of human civilization upon the earth. Therefore, we cannot be so picky and say He was talking to a particular son of Canaan, etc. He is talking to the Hamitic man!

Let me point out here that most often the 28th chapter of Ezekiel is said to be talking about none other than Lucifer. I am convinced that this chapter not only talks about Lucifer, but it also talks about the black man, the highly exalted, Afro-Asiatic man whom God raised up to be the founder of human civilization many eons ago. It was some three thousand years before Christ.

God is also talking about Lucifer, *"the anointed cherub that covereth."* He covered the mercy seat with his wings in heaven. He was the chief praise leader in heaven, but Eden was not in heaven. Eden was on the earth. Eden was in Africa. As a matter of fact, Eden was another name for Africa, that pleasant land, that delightsome land.

> *"And the Lord God planted a garden eastward in Eden…"* (Genesis 2:8a)

Or eastward in Africa. It was in East Africa, in Tanzania. In verse 14 of Ezekiel 28, God says:

> *"I established you (talking to the king of Tyre, that black Canaanite king) and you were in the holy mountain of God."* (NKJV)

In other words, in the very early stages of humankind on earth, Adam was a man of color, and he walked and talked with God.

God's Plan for the Sons of Ham

After the flood, God started the human population over again through the three sons of Noah: Shem, Ham and Japheth. I want you to know that all three of them knew God. But the most outstanding of them, the one who superseded the others in that day and hour, was none other than the offspring of Ham! They walked with God. Ezekiel 28:15 says:

> "You walked back and forth in the midst of the fiery stones, you were perfect in your ways from the day you were created, till iniquity was found in you." (NKJV)

Iniquity was found in Adam, iniquity was found in Lucifer, iniquity was found in that super-genius, Hamitic people whom God used in the beginning of human civilization. Now God is talking to this Sidonian king. He says:

> "By multitude of your trading you became filled with violence and sinned. Therefore, I cast as a profane thing out of the mountain of God and I destroyed you...from the midst of the fiery stones. Your heart was lifted up because of your beauty.
> You corrupted your wisdom for the sake of your splendor." (NKJV)

The beauty of the ancient Ethiopians, Nubians and others from that period of time was really their wisdom. This is what the Greeks marveled at.

Isaiah 18, speaks of these smooth-skinned people. The commentators of the *Spirit-Filled Life Bible* called this a proclamation against Ethiopians, but I don't think this is Ethiopia, having been there recently. I checked the maps out and found that these were the Sudanese people; these were the people who had called the Nubians, who lived in the southern part of Egypt. They were very black and beautiful people and the ones who were the founders of great inventions by their great wisdom. The Egyptians got their foundation from them. Isaiah 18:1 says:

> *Woe to the land shadowed with buzzing wings, which is beyond the rivers of Ethiopia.*

This refers to the two branches of the Nile, the Blue Nile and the White Nile, The Blue Nile originates in Uganda, and the White Nile originates in Ethiopia. They come together or converge in the Sudan. In the city called Khartoum, Sudan, the two branches become one river, the Nile, which flows into Egypt, until it empties into the Mediterranean Sea. The Nile River is the longest river system in the world. So, God says "woe" to these people and in verse seven He says:

> *"In that time a present will be brought to the Lord of hosts from a people tall and smooth of skin and a people terrible from their beginning onward, a people powerful and treading down."*

God's Plan for the Sons of Ham

The people of Sudan (Nubia) were great bowman, great archers. I believe that tradition goes back to Nimrod, the mighty hunter, the mighty archer and bowman before the Lord, and a mighty warrior. God says of these beautiful black people that they were tall and of a smooth skin, and a people terrible from their beginning onward, a nation powerful and treading down. They were a mighty warring people, a people who were mighty in warfare:

"Whose land the rivers divide to the place of the name of the Lord of hosts, to Mt. Zion." (Isaiah 18:7b)

The two rivers come together at Khartoum (in the Sudan) and then begin to flow as one river, which is the River Nile. I believe God is talking about the people of the Sudan, which are *beyond the rivers* of Ethiopia, the two branches of the Nile, the Blue and the White Nile. What I am trying to say then is that these people from antiquity were great and mighty and very wise. They wrought great things in the earth, and they became lifted up because of their pride.

Again, what are we saying? We are saying both secular (humanistic) and sacred (biblical) sources agree that the black man was highly blessed, exalted and used by God to lay the very foundations of human (Western) civilization, and that his accomplishments were astounding, and that many lay hidden under the "sands of time" in Egypt. We are saying that the accomplishments of these dark-skinned geniuses were lately rediscovered in the 18th century by Europeans, who claimed these great feats as their own!

We are, for the most part, in agreement with the historical, anthropological and archeological writings of our illustrious African fathers, either of the motherland, America or the Diaspora. However, we believe the Bible gives the more accurate reason for the downfall of Kemet, Nubia, etc., i.e.: they violated one of the Lord's great principles, *"He that exalteth himself shall be abased,"* and he who fails to give God the glory due unto his name, shall be humiliated (Luke 18:14b).

Please refer the book of Daniel, chapter 4 and verses 29 through 37 for an example of the second principle cited above which was fulfilled in Nebuchadnezzar king of Babylon and king of kings. Because of boasting pridefully in himself and taking credit for his great accomplishments and failing to give the glory to the Most High God, the true God above all gods, he was smitten with insanity and humiliated—to become like a brute beast for seven years, crawling on all fours and eating grass like an ox! Could it be that God allowed a similar fate to befall the sons of Ham who in the beginning of mankind were endowed by their Creator with superlative genius, wisdom and ability to lay the foundations of Western Civilization, in all of the major disciplines, and accomplishments of modern, civilized man? Did they, like king Nebuchadnezzar, exalt themselves to be like God, robbing him of His glory, praise and honor, and giving it to another? Is this why we, their offspring, have endured such suffering, deprivation, injury and humiliation?

Could the Apostle Paul (a dark-skinned man, Acts 21:37-38) be referring to the ancient Kemetic people when he wrote:

> "For the wrath of God is manifested from heaven against all ungodliness and unrighteousness of men, who hold the truth in unrighteousness because that which may be known of God is (was) revealed in them?" (Romans 1:19)

In November, 1986, while attending the dedication of a great church in Benin City. Nigeria (the great miracle Cathedrome) a certain noted, white, T.V. minister from America, stood in the pulpit before fifty thousand people. (The church seats about fifteen to twenty thousand, and there were many more thousands on the outside). Reverend Kenneth Copeland made the following bold statement about the Black man: "The black man is the strongest man upon the face of the earth!" It has been Kenneth Copeland, along with Dr. Oral Roberts, one of the great fathers of Pentecostal and Charismatic Christians in "America and around the world, who have openly declared that the next mighty move of God by his Holy Spirit upon the earth shall be led by men of color, by **black** men!

Basically, we are pointing out that because Egypt

became exalted, and because Sidon became exalted, as well as other ancient people of color, in that God used them to establish the foundation of human civilization, i.e., (Western civilization), God had to bring them down through humiliation.

God's Plan for the Sons of Ham

CHAPTER ELEVEN
CONTEMPORARY TRENDS IN RESTORATION

Now, let us turn our attention to contemporary trends in politics, in society, in the church, in America and in Africa—with respect to people of color.

Whereas we began writing this book in 1994, it is now 1996, and there is an historic event that occurred last year that we must speak of in this writing. That event was none other than the march in Washington, D.C. by nearly one million African-American men hailed as the "Million Man March." This "March" which was organized by and headed up by Nation of Islam leader, Minister Louis Farrakhan, was a statement of self-worth, justice and "atonement" for nearly one million Black men and their sons.

The March was not only historic, because it was the largest rally or gathering of its kind in the nation's capital in the history of America. It was proof that African Americans can work together for a common cause!

The March, including the speeches by various Black church leaders, had a positive, inspirational and uplifting effect on black people there and throughout the U. S. and abroad.

This author saw fit to write to Farrakhan and commend him on the March and its positive effects. We also took occasion to witness to him about the necessity of being truly born-again by the Spirit of God. We invite our readers to join in praying for Minister Farrakhan to be saved, so that his strenuous efforts to elevate the level of the Black man around the world will be of **eternal value.**

It is no secret, and I say this without apology or fear of contradiction, the people of color have simply been tolerated by whites and others throughout the world, and in America, since time immemorial! Our fathers were looked upon as "darkies," and strong, brute, "beasts of burden." Our mothers were looked upon as available sex objects and "mammies." Few gave us credit for having brains at all, but some of the greatest inventions in the history of this nation were creations of burnt-face people: open heart surgery, blood plasma, and the traffic light, just to name a few.

I say to our white brethren in the church, "Move over, and make room for us; for our time has surely come!" We must realize that none of us came here to stay, and that nothing remains the same forever—not even *white supremacy!* It is time that you open your eyes and see, and open your ears and hear the Lord shouting in this hour:

"Princes (royal leaders) are coming out of Egypt (Ham or sun-burnt people); (and) Ethiopia (people of the burnt face) is stretching forth her hands unto God." (Psalm 68:31)

Look around yourself and see a Dr. Martin Luther King leading his people out of degradation and indignities and receiving the Nobel Peace Prize. Open your eyes and see a Nelson Mandela rising from twenty-five years of imprisonment for standing up and resisting Satan's apartheid system of dehumanizing degradation, to become the first black president of South Africa in over three hundred years! Wake up and see a son of Ham rising to our nation's highest military office as Chairman of the Joints Chiefs of Staff, even General Colin Powell, who has been touted as a possible presidential candidate. See Ron Brown, the first black Chairman of the Democratic Party and first black U.S. Secretary of Commerce.

The elevation of the Black man today may be likened unto the experiences of Esther and Mordecai in the Bible, in the book of Esther. Esther, an orphan Jewish girl, and

Mordecai her uncle, were leftover captives in foreign land, i.e., Babylon, and later Persia. They existed in Persia as second class citizens; but in God's appointed time Esther became the Queen of Persia and uncle Mordecai became Prime Minister of the land.

A further example of God's elevation of the sons of Ham in America today may be seen in the case of Prudential Insurance Company's number one salesman. I am told that this person, an African who is also a born-again, Spirit-filled Christian, attained the position of number one salesman in Prudential in December, 1995.

The brother, who is member of Dr. Larry Lea's church in San Diego, is said to have attained this phenomenal feat through divine intervention. It is said that our brother sold 117 million dollars worth of insurance for Prudential in seven days! This accomplishment is said to have prompted an investigation of this Black super salesman by the Securities and Exchange Commission, an investigation allegedly ordered by the president of the company.

One of the greatest Christian revivals in world history is taking in place on the continent of Africa at this time and it is in the country of Nigeria. Massive crusades involving hundreds of thousands of souls are the order of the day. Let us not overlook a country like Ghana where the same kind of awesome move of the Holy Ghost is taking place.

It has been said that the Gospel has come "full circle."

As the Gospel was *first* exported to Africa from Israel in the beginning of the church age, (Acts 8:27-39), so the Gospel has today *returned* to Africa in a mighty way. Surely:

> *"Princes shall (have) come out of Egypt (Kemet) and Ethiopia (Africa) shall soon (suddenly) stretch forth her hands unto God."* (Psalm 68:31)

It's happening now!

Let us turn our attention back to the U.S.A. Without a doubt the Lord is responding to the cries of the seed of Ham in America and is favoring us with His hand of blessing. The June, 1995 issue of Charisma Magazine cites the mighty move of God in African American churches in an article entitled, "Shoutin' it from the Housetops." The caption on the cover says "Black churches across America are stirring souls and transforming cities." The referenced article, by B. Denise Hawkins, opens by saying:

> "Electrifying fervor is surging through America's black churches. But this Pentecostal revival is more than soul-stirring gospel music. It just might transform entire cities for Jesus."

She goes on to say in the article:

> *"It will be a busy day at Full Gospel A.M.E. Zion*

Church in Temple Hills, Maryland, with 17,000 members every month...Cherry's church (the church previously mentioned) represents a fascinating trend. It is one of many black denominational churches that has been affected in recent years by a sweeping neo-Pentecostal movement.

Today, churches in the huge National Baptist Convention USA (NBCUSA) and the African Methodist Episcopal Church – as well as Cherry's AME Zion Church—are being invigorated by a new emphasis on personal spirituality, Bible teaching, family renewal, evangelism and aggressive social action."

Wake up my fair-skinned brethren and smell the "Roses of Truth" which are blooming everywhere. I say again, since 1947, your world rule has been coming to an end. Your time in the sun is just about up, despite Teddy Roosevelt's and Woodrow Wilson's declaration of (the white man's) "Manifest Destiny," that is, to rule the world.

This was the cry of Japheth all over the world during his days of colonialism and domination of all who did not look like him. The Dutch, British, France, Spanish and Portuguese alike practically overran each other to see who could subjugate the greatest numbers of peoples of the world---Africans, East Indians, islanders and Native Americans. But the sun always (now) sets on what used to be the great British and other Caucasian empires. It is time to realize that we sons of Africa, whose forefathers founded human civilization, are not, nor have ever been the "white man's burden." After, all we did not extract ourselves out of Africa to be forcibly brought to the New World. We were brought in chains against our wills! Some well-intentioned Caucasians who went to the "dark continent" years ago did help some, but did more exploiting of the people and the land, than helping them.

We must realize that the God of all justice, who sits high and looks low, who lifts up one, and pulls down another, is saying;

> *It is time for my sons of color to once again be set in places of prominence. They have served their time of humiliation and punishment for their sins.*

I hear the Lord saying through Isaiah His prophet:

> "**Blessed** *be Egypt (Ham) my people!*" (Isaiah 19:25)

I hear Him saying again:

> "*Comfort, ye comfort my people…Speak comfortably… and cry out to her, that her warfare is ended, that her iniquity is pardoned; For she has received from the Lord's hand double for all of her sins.*"
> (Isaiah 40:1-2)

Jesus made us know that there will be some of the most unlikely people entering the kingdom of God ahead of others. In St. Matthew 21:31, Jesus said:

> *"Assuredly, I say to you that tax collectors (publicans) and harlots enter the kingdom of God before you."* (NKJV)

It is sad that Blacks have often been thought of as less than the categories of people whom Jesus referenced above who would enter the kingdom before others, who thought themselves to be superior. Again in St. Matthew 21:43 Jesus said:

> *"Therefore the kingdom of God will be taken from you and given to a nation bearing the fruits of it."* (NKJV)

CHAPTER TWELVE
THESE ARE NO CONCIDENCES!

At this junction we would like to refer to other clear evidences of the Lord elevating the sons of Ham and restoring them to places of prominence in the Church, as well as in the world today.

Having mentioned several persons of color who reached high levels of achievement and prominence in politics, business, the military, etc.; in the USA, in our first printing, we want to cite more examples of the same in both the spiritual and secular arenas in this second printing.

During the 90's some of the most sought-after preachers/teachers of color in the U.S. and around the world have been names like Bishop T.D. Jakes, Dr. Myles Munroe, Bishop Paul Morton, Evangelist Jackie

McCullough, et.al.

In the church music arena, we have such stellar psalmists as Ron Kenoly, Alvin Slaughter and Donnie McClurkin, who are inspiring huge multicultural audiences. These brethren have reached the very top of their professions! The same could be said of Bebe and Cece Winans, Larnell Harris, as well as a cross over singer like <u>Whitney Houston</u>.

I believe it is an interesting observation that <u>percentage wise</u>, in the U.S., there are more mega-churches pastored by men of color than of any other ethnic group. When we consider churches like Full Gospel AME Zion pastored by Dr. John Cherry with upwards of 18,000 members or pastors like Pastor Creflo Dollar, Bishop Eddie Long, Bishop Charles Blake, Dr. Fred Price and many other with 15,000 or more members, we have to declare loudly, that <u>these are no coincidences</u>!

When we turn our attention to the continent of Africa (the Land of Ham) the picture becomes more startling of God's hand resting upon the sons of Ham in a special way in this hour. Without an ounce of exaggeration, we note that 10,000 member congregations on this continent are becoming commonplace. As we mentioned earlier in this book, we know bishops and pastors in Africa personally who pastor churches of 10,000-20,000+members. The Most Reverend Archbishop Benson Idahosa, my own spiritual covering, oversees several millions of believers in several thousand churches.

These Are No Coincidences!

We know of an archbishop in Kenya who pastors a congregation of 50,000 believers. His name is Reverend Ezekiel Guti. We sit together on the Board of Trustees of the International Third World Leadership Association, under the Directorship of Dr. Myles Munroe. Additionally, I have read of a Protestant church in Nigeria with 75,000-100,000 members; and I have also read a Roman Catholic Cathedral in Abijan, Nigeria that is a replica of St. Peter's Basilica in Rome-and rivals it in size and cost!

Again, my beloveds, these trends are by no means the result of coincidences! God's hand is in the plan! When we turn our attention to the field of professional sports in the U.S., it again becomes apparent that the sons of Ham have been and are being raised to places of prominence! In the major sports of baseball, basketball and football, some of the highest salaries are going to athletes of color. Michael Jordon has come to define professional basketball in the U.S.A. The sons of Ham could have starred, especially in professional baseball in this country many years ago- if we had been given the opportunity sooner! But thanks be to God, our time has come! It would be futile to begin to name names because they are so numerous and predominant in these sports. The same could be said for the heavyweight division of the sport of boxing.

Thank God a born-again, Spirit-filled Christian currently holds the title, in the person of Brother Evander Holyfield! In April 1997, the young African-American-

Thai sensation named Tiger Woods won the U.S. Masters PGA Golf tournament, smashing all previous records for the lowest score in the Tournament's history, and winning it as the youngest champion ever! We are seeing Isaiah 19:25 fulfilled before our very eyes! God is indeed saying, "Blessed be Egypt (Ham) my people!"

Finally, let us take a brief look at the entertainment field where talk show host Oprah Winfrey is the undisputed champion of salary earners; for men or women, black or white or otherwise. Names like Bill Cosby, Quincy Jones and Denzel Washington present stellar examples of God's hand resting mightily upon the sons (and daughters) of Ham to raise them to places of prominence and to be leaders in their crafts in this hour.

Time would fail me to talk about persons of color like Dr. Carson, master surgeons, at the world renown Johns Hopkins Hospital in Baltimore, Maryland, and others of his caliber! We repeat dear readers, that, "These are no coincidences!" This is the moving of the sovereign hand of God in the affairs of men to fulfill His original, intended purposes. After all, it was the Lord Jesus Christ Himself, God in human form, who declared in St. Matthew's Gospel, chapter twenty, "The last shall be first, and the first shall be last." Surely, He who created all and is Lord of all knows His own business, and does all things "After the counsel of His own will" (Eph. 1:11).

CHAPTER THIRTEEN
HAM—HELPER OF GOD'S PEOPLE

Before we conclude this book, allow us to chronicle from the Bible the fact that the sons of Ham have historically been involved in helping the people of Israel. In Joshua chapter two we find Rahab a Canaanite harlot risking her life to hide the Israelite spies who had entered Jericho to spy out the land. Her act of heroism saved their lives. She was a daughter of Ham.

In 2 Samuel chapter 18 we find a Cushite (a son of Cush, thus a son of Ham) who wisely delivered David the news of the death of his son Absalom. When Ahimaaz, the son of the Jewish priest Zadok, ran ahead of the Cushite to David, but had not eyewitness message to report. David told him to *"stand aside."*

When Jeremiah was cast into a dungeon into quicksand

for prophesying the word of the Lord against Jerusalem to king Zedekiah and his princes, he would have died of hunger and suffocation had it not been for the bold and heroic stand of a black man, Ebed-Melech, the Ethiopian eunuch! He went to the king and pleaded for Jeremiah's life and the king granted him the right to rescue Jeremiah from certain death in that dungeon (Jeremiah 38:6-13).

The spirit of helpfulness in the sons of Ham toward the children of Israel reached its zenith in the case of the Black man who helped Jesus bear His cruel cross en route to Golgotha. The word of the Lord reads thusly:

> *"Now as they led Him (Jesus) away, they (the Roman, Gentile soldiers) laid hold of a certain mam, Simon a Cyrenian (a North African), who was coming from the country, and on him they laid the cross that he might bear it after Jesus."* (Luke 23:26)

Surely:

> *"God is not unjust to forget your (our) labor of love which you (we) have shown toward His name, in that you (we) have ministered to the saints and do minister."* (Hebrews 6:10)

People of color for years have been excluded from white churches as members; and where we have been accepted in some congregations, it's been in menial, lesser positions.

For the most part, we have been used as singers or ushers. This is not true in every integrated church congregation in America today. Your author was invited to minister in an all-white congregation in Baltimore in the 60s. I was a pastor and had been preaching for ten years! Yet I was asked by one of their church leaders, "What do you do?" As though I was expected to sing, tap dance or perform some other act of entertainment! I did what all preachers do, I *preached!*

> *Racism releases the spirit of death from one culture onto another. In the face of this satanic world ruler, God is opening the floodgates of His River of Life; He shall bring healing to the nations. Indeed, even now, in the House of the Lord the phrase 'white church', "black church' is being banished forever.*
>
> *You cannot pick up a news magazine without finding an article on racism. The need for reconciliation and healing between races surfaces in nearly every form of media. It cries for attention and healing. Racism is complex and a sensitive issue. Yet, the healing of our cities will not occur until the church is delivered of cultural pride and insolence and has, itself, become a source of healing…"*
>
> *Therefore, regardless of your ethnic background, we entreat you to stay soft and open toward God. It is likely that old wounds shall resurface, and yesterday's fears and opinions rekindle. However, as the Lord is*

granting us grace, let us walk forward together toward Christ's healing. (The Original African Heritage Study Bible, p.85)

CHAPTER FOURTEEN
HAM BLESSED, CANAAN CURSED

Prior to closing we would be remiss if we failed to mention a "great man" in the Bible who appeared as a man of color, as well as some noted men of color who made great contributions in the establishment of the church. The "great man" mentioned above is none other than Melchizedek, king of Salem, priest of the Most High God! He was greater than Abram; he blessed him, serving him bread and wine, and received tithes of Abram. Hebrews 7:4 and 7 bear witness to my statement above.

Melchizedek, whose name means *king of righteousness* and *king of peace,* was not only greater than Abraham, but he was a high ranking angelic, supernatural being who appeared in human form as a black Canaanite king! See

Hebrew 7:1-10 and Genesis 14:8 for confirmation of my statement above.

Did not Noah in a "hung over" state curse Canaan with servanthood to his brothers, and bless Japheth to "dwell in the tents of Shem?" Here comes another irony. I submit that the facts contained in the Bible will show that God did not honor that curse nor the blessing spoken by Noah in any thorough way. The facts are that some Canaanites were made servants, but others were highly blessed and greatly used by God. Examples of some highly blessed Canaanites are Melchizedek, Rahab the harlot, and Bathsheba, the wife of king David and mother of Solomon, the wisest and wealthiest of all Judean kings. Let us not forget the widow of Zarpheth who fed Elijah.

With regard to Noah's misdirected blessing upon Japheth, the scriptures clearly show that it was Ham who *"dwelleth in the tents of Shem,"* not Japheth! We repeat, the concubines of Abraham were Hagar and Keturah, both of whom descended from Ham. Esau married Hittite and Ishmaelite wives. Joseph married Asenath, an Egyptian (Hamitic) woman. Judah married a Canaanite woman. Likewise, David married a daughter out of Ham, Bathsheba. Of a truth it was Ham in whom Noah's pronounced blessing was fulfilled, not Japheth!

Allow us to reference some men of color in the new Testament who were highly regarded by and used by God. First of all, there was Simon the Cyrenian (Of North Africa): *"On him they laid the cross that he might bear it after Jesus"* (Luke 23:26). Then there was "A man of Ethiopia, a eunuch of great authority" (Secretary of the treasury) who was saved and declared the gospel of Christ in Africa *first,* before it was preached in Europe or Asia. (Acts 8:26-59 39) Finally, there were prophets and teachers at the church at Antioch such as *"Simeon who called Niger (dark or black), (and) Lucius of Cyrene..."* who were among those who ordained (laid hands on) Paul and Barnabas as apostles of Jesus Christ (Acts 13:1-2).

God's Plan for the Sons of Ham

CHAPTER FIFTEEN
BLACK CHAMPIONS OF THE CHURCH

Finally, allow us to name a few of the great early church champions who were men of color. We shall draw upon information in a book entitled, *Blacks Who Died for Jesus,* by Mark Hyman, journalist-historian.

Mark Hyman called Origen, the "Black Bible Expert." Origen was one of the early thinkers of the Christian church. He was born in 185 A.D. in the Nile Valley (Nubian) region, and later migrated to Egypt. Early on, Origen became the head of the Christian training school in Alexandria Egypt.

As you may already know, Alexandria was the world's earliest educational center, where universities, libraries and the wisdom of the ancient people of Egypt (Africa) was taught and preserved. Alexandria flourished as a center for the study of theology, philosophy and other disciplines as noted in Acts 18:24, where the eloquent Jew named Apollos was cited, who was born in Alexandria and was *"mighty in the Scriptures."*

One of Origen's achievement was his writing of six thousand books:

> *Learned in Greek philosophy. Origen is still the greatest Bible scholar to ever have applied to the Christian Church... (he) was a vital part of the foundation and the fabric of what the great Christian Church was to become.*

The second black Champion of the early church was none other than Tertullian (A.D. 150 230). Born in Carthage (North Africa), the son of a Roman Centurion and apparently an African mother. It is said of Tertullian that "he gave the church Latin and wrote the first Exposition of the Lord's prayer in any language. "This giant of the early church was highly trained in law. He became an expert and became a Christian in A.D. 193.

> *Tertullian was the first Christian theologian to leave behind an extensive collection of works written in Latin... He was the first to introduce the special idiom of Latin-speaking Christians into literature.*
>
> *Tertullian never tried to create a theological system but he often found formulas and definitions which*

were clear and precise, particularly in his doctrine of the Trinity. His doctrine of the Trinity finds its best expression in the late work Adversus Praxen (after 213) and it is the doctrine (and in Christianity) that he made his greatest contribution in theology.*

Our third Black general of the early church is Saint Cyprian, a great African bishop:

Cyprian was a Black native of Carthage. He came into the church an accomplished man. He was a lawyer, a protégé of Tertullian, and he taught rhetoric at the University of Carthage. He was an African nobleman, middle-aged and wealthy. In A.D. 248, soon, after his baptism, Cyprian was ordained a priest. From that point he remained forever a dedicated leader in the African Church.

Cyprian played a prominent role in the history of the Roman Church. He was later elevated to the Bishop of Carthage and became primate of all of Africa...With intense vigor Cyprian promoted African participation at high levels in the African Church...Cyprian is considered one of the great African writers in the entire church history.

Our fourth and most prominent Black champion of the early church is the inimitable Augustine, "Pillar of the Church."

Some writers and historians, inside and outside the church, have debated bitterly over the race of Saint Augustine. Sometimes the argument overshadowed the great work Augustine performed for the church and the fact that he has become the accepted father of theology...Augustine was an African of Nubian stock...He was educated at a Black university, the University of Carthage; and Carthage was a Black nation in Northeast Africa...

The religious writings of Augustine have become literary and spiritual monuments to the creative greatness of the bishop. The Predestination of the Saints and the Gift of Perseverance were among his first books. During his lifetime he wrote 90 books. The Confessions and The City of God are the most renowned. He has justly been called the father of theology, or the inventor of the study of religion. These writings covered an enormous range of subjects such as morals, history, philosophy and heresy to name a few. The Christian churches throughout the world have used Augustine's books as major references.

The theological views of Augustine held sway in Roman Catholic church for about one thousand years, until the theological emphases of St. Thomas Aquinas superseded his.

While speaking of" Champions of the Church" of African descent, we must include a Champion of the modern-day church. That person is none other than Reverend William "Daddy" Seymour. Without any exaggeration whatever, Rev. William Seymour is indisputable the "Father of Modern-day Pentecostalism"! He was that one-eyed, Black preacher whom God chose to be the leader and pastor of the "Apostolic Faith Gospel Mission" on Azusa Street in Los Angeles, California. It was he who was in charge of the mission where the world witnessed the mightiest, nascent outpouring and move of the Holy Spirit in this century!

That sovereign move of God lasted continuously for three and a half years (1906-1909) in a former horse stable. Believers and sinners came from around the world to behold or share in this modern-day, unprecedented, divine phenomenon! Most who came received the glorious outpouring or baptism with the Holy Spirit, as recorded in Acts 2:4; 10;44-46 and 19:1-6. Many received miraculous healings and other miraculous blessings. It is said that angels appeared in the hay lofts and serenaded the saints with the most glorious, heavenly music since they appeared to the shepherds announcing Christ's birth. Revival services were conducted three times a day, seven days a week for three and a half years, without cessation!

The Black Christian actor, Leon Isaacs Kennedy, in May of 1995, presented a video documentary on the Trinity Broad-casting Network about the Azusa Street Revival. One of the videos on the life and ministry of Reverend William "Daddy" Seymour does a beautiful job of setting the record straight, and giving to this great Black Christian leader the honor and respect rightly due him. It is entitled "From Tragedy to Triumph!"

The *tragedy* was that white Pentecostal church leaders in Reverend Seymour's day refused to accept his New Testament message and practice of love, unity and equality of all believers in the Body of Christ, yea, the Church! They plotted and schemed against this humble, godly, gentle man of God, padlocked him out of his own church, and carried off the vast majority of his large congregation, his board members and the church's mailing list. After humiliating this chosen servant of God in the most obnoxious manner (obviously because they could not accept his leadership as a Black man) they ostracized and shunned him and charged him with being "an unfit church leader," because he chose to marry.

The *triumph* is that the Pentecostal movement (in modern times) has lasted nearly a century. Today it is alive and well and growing more robustly than any other Christian movement around the world. Honest Christian theology professors, who happen to be white, from major Christian institutions of higher learning, openly concur in the aforementioned video, that modern Pentecostalism owes its existence to the Azusa Street Revival, and the *undeniable,* divinely chosen leadership of a Black, one-eyed preacher named William Seymour!

Let us open our eyes and see the consistency of God! He began human civilization with the sons of Ham. A son of Ham assisted in the founding of Christianity i.e., Simon of Cyrene, a North African, who helped Jesus carry his cross! In the apostolic church, there were sons of Ham in the church of Antioch, prophets and teachers, who laid hands on Saul of Tarsus and Barnabas, and ordained them as Christ's apostles! And the Gospel was preached (after Judea and Samaria) in Africa, first, before it was heard in Europe!

Finally, in this 20th century, the Lord initiated the mightiest move of His Holy Spirit on earth in a humble horse stable, under the leadership of another son of Ham, Reverend William Seymour. Even though Brother Seymour was despised and rejected by his Japhethic brethren (due to jealously, no doubt) thank God he is getting his due respect albeit some eighty-six years late! *"Shall not the Judge of all the earth do right?"* (Genesis 18:25a). Undeniably! Yes! Yes! Yes!

God's Plan for the Sons of Ham

CHAPTER SIXTEEN
THREE AFRICAN POPES

Before we can conclude this section, we must recognize the three African popes who ruled the Church in Rome.

ST. VICTOR

More and more staggering facts are coming to the forefront about Blacks in the history of the Christian Church. One of the most explosive is proof that three Africans headed the church as popes between the second and fifth centuries. Each made contributions which were as significant and lasting as did any of the others. Less than two hundred years after the death of Jesus, African-born Victor was elected Pope. He was the last Pope of the second century (A.D. 189-199. He carried a Latin name as most Africans did at that time. As Pope, his reign was full of controversy. One of the conflicts arose over the true date of Easter. The Asiatic church severely criticized Pope Victor because he opposed their celebration of Easter on the fourteenth day after the Vernal Equinox, regardless of the day on which it fell. Victor ended the matter by deciding to celebrate Easter on the Sunday following the fourteenth day of Vernal Equinox. Churches everywhere obeyed the Pope's edict, except the churches in Asia Minor. Victor was declared a martyr of the church even though he died a natural death...St. Victor is buried in St. Peter's Basilica in Vatican City in Rome. He lies next to St. Peter, the first Pope.

MILITIADES

Militiades, a Black priest from Africa, was elected the thirty-seventh Pope in A.D. 311. This African Church leader was first to have an official residence. Emperor Constantine's wife gave him the luxurious Lateran Palace...

A split came about within the church after Constantine began to meddle in Church affairs...Militiades was asked by the emperor to preside over a series of controversies and debates.

A synod was convened in the great Lateran Palace. This was the first such council ever presided over by a pope with the blessings of government. In attendance were fifteen Italian bishops and three from France. It was Militiades who finally brought the church to victory over Rome.

GELASIUS

Gelasius was born in Rome of African parents. They lived comfortably. He received a superior education. In his youth he was a member of Roman clergy. As Pope, he accomplished many significant things. Gelasius arranged several rules for the clergy. He ordered that the revenue of the church should be divided into four parts: one part for bishops, one part for the clergy, one part for the poor and one part to support the churches and divine services. He tried to uproot a major competing religion called Manichaeism…Gelasius has been recognized as one on the most vigorous, resourceful and efficient popes in the fifth century (492-496). His writings and sermons have been quoted down through the ages. He has been praised for his plain life. His concern for the poor was outstanding.

His many songs and writings have been lost in time. It is believed by many present-day Catholics that Gelasian The Sacrementary was written by him…In fact, Gelasius was the first Pope to seriously advocate the complete separation of church and state. Gelasius is also known for his truth which he explained to a council of bishops in

Rome. He said that the Lord told St. Peter, when he made him head of the church, every pope as St. Peter's successor was to be head of the church and was to hold supreme power over all of the churches.

Oh, pity of pities and wonder of wonders, that there have been so many deceptions and conspiracies against the sable-skin people from Africa in European history since the late 1700s! Once again, we say the truth: The Black man's contributions in the world and in the church have been hidden for centuries under the debris of lies!

Having received my Master's in Theology and having done my doctoral studies in that field at St. Mary's Seminary and University in Baltimore, Maryland, I am most appalled that no professor ever once mentioned the blackness of the champions of the early church we have just cited. What a travesty! especially since St. Mary's is the oldest seminary in the United State of America! It is a highly revered and recognized school of higher learning.

CHAPTER SEVENTEEN
CONCLUSION

With this said, let us move toward the conclusion of our book. Of a truth, as the old saying goes, "Truth crushed to the ground shall rise again," and so it is these latter days. The truth about God's "earth-colored" sons, however distorted in the past, is being uncovered today. And that truth is indeed rising again! In this End Time, God is indeed calling Egypt (the Black man) Blessed, according to Isaiah 19:25.

Is it not ironic that much of the known "history" of the world has portrayed the Black man as lowly and inferior when compared to others? Awaken, my Caucasian brethren, and know that Jesus counts us as your *equals* (Matthew 20:12). He is saying that it is time for the despised and rejected sons of Ham to take their rightful place in Him and in His church! He says:

> *"Is it not lawful for me to do what I wish with my own? Or is your eye evil because I am good? So the last shall be first, and the first last. For many are called, but few are chosen."* (Matthew 20:15-16 NKJV)

Please be advised that:

> *"God has chosen the base (insignificant and lowly) things which are not (nothing) to bring to nothing the things that are, that no flesh should glory in His presence."* (I Corinthians 1:28-29 NKJV)

So, we close with the inspiring song (The Negro National Anthem) of the inimitable poet, James Weldon Johnson:

> *Lift every voice and sing,*
> *'til earth and heaven ring,*
> *Ring with the harmony of liberty,*
> *Let its resounding rise,*
> *High as the listening skies,*
> *Let us march on 'til victory is won.*
> *Sing a song, full of the faith that*
> *That dark past has taught us,*
> *Sing a song, full of hope that the present*
> *has brought us,*
> *Facing the rising sun,*

Conclusion

of a new day begun,
Let us march on 'til victory is won.

Let us look beyond the two hundred and fifty years of slavery and one hundred and thirty years of discrimination and oppression since, which predisposed our people to such social aberrations as drugs abuse, wholesale killings, proliferation of out-of-wedlock teen-age mothers, fatherless homes etc., to a brighter future.

Facing the rising sun,
of a new day begun,
Let us march on 'til victory is won.

Selah

BIBLIOGRAPHY

- *Bible, Spirit Filled Life,* New King James Version, Nashville, TN: *Thomas Nelson Publishers,* 1991
- Browder, Anthony T. *Nile Valley Contribution to Civilization, Exploding the Myths, Volume I,* Washington D.C.; The Institute of Karmic Guidance, 1992
- Emanuel, William Gilbert, *People of Color in the Bible*
- Herodotus, *The History of Herodotus,* Translated by George Rawlinson, New York, NY: Tudor Publishing Co., 1939
- *Holy Bible, Original African Heritage Edition,* King James Version, Nashville, TN: The James C. Winston Publishing Company, 1993
- Hyman, Mark, *Blacks Who Died for Jesus.*
- *Illustrated Dictionary & Concordance of the Bible,* The Readers Digest Association, Inc.
- Johnson, John L. *The Black Biblical Heritage,* Winston-Derek Publishers, Inc.
- Kennedy, Leon Isaac, *From Tragedy to Triumph*
- Roger, J.A. *Your History from the Beginning to the Present,* Baltimore, MD: Black Classics Press, 1983
- *Smith's Bible Dictionary,* Nashville, TN; Holman Bible Publishers, 1989
- Unger, Merrill F., *Unger's Bible Dictionary,* Chicago, IL: Moody Press, 1987

- Volney, C.F. *The Ruins of Empires,* Baltimore, MD: Black Classics Press, 1990

www.ingramcontent.com/pod-product-compliance
Lightning Source LLC
Chambersburg PA
CBHW072037110526
44592CB00012B/1461